D1600477

Between Man and Woman

Between Man and Woman

The Dynamics of Intersexual Relationships

Everett Shostrom
James Kavanaugh

NASH PUBLISHING
Los Angeles

LIBRARY OF CONGRESS CATALOG CARD NUMBER: 70-143020
STANDARD BOOK NUMBER: 8402-1175-9

PUBLISHED SIMULTANEOUSLY IN THE UNITED STATES AND
CANADA BY NASH PUBLISHING, 9255 SUNSET BOULEVARD,
LOS ANGELES, CALIFORNIA 90069.

PRINTED IN THE UNITED STATES OF AMERICA

FIRST PRINTING

To Donna and Pat

Acknowledgments

The authors are grateful to the theorists whose research provided important foundations for many of the ideas in this book. We would like to mention particularly the seminal work of Robert Winch, Virginia Satir and Don Jackson. Also the work of Lederer, Watzlawick, and Beavin, and the work of Leary, Coffey, and Barron from the Kaiser Foundation Psychology Research Project at Berkeley.

Since our book is co-authored, each of us has a particular and personal acknowledgment to make. Everett L. Shostrom is singularly grateful to his teachers, Abraham Maslow and Frederick Perls, and to the Staff of the Institute of Therapeutic Psychology — Robert

Hilton, Evalyn E. DiDomenico, Alan Levy and Neil Matheson. Robert Hilton was especially helpful to him with theoretical suggestions. Wayne Zimmerman and Robert Knapp were especially helpful in the construction of The Pair Attraction and Love Attraction Inventories.

James Kavanaugh is especially grateful to his teachers, who led him from the world of theology to psychology; to Philip R. Kavanaugh, his brother, a brilliant theorist, who will see much of himself in this book; to Carl Rogers, a courageous pioneer and friend, who convinced him that psychologists could be beautiful; to Everett Shostrom, a co-author and friend, a tireless researcher and innovator; to William Brockley and to Keery Merwin.

To Mary Stuttle, we are grateful for her tireless efficiency in typing of the manuscript.

We are also grateful to our students at United States International University, and to our clients, who have trusted us with their lives and hopes.

Contents

Part One
Man and Woman

9

Part Two
Love Attraction Inventory

Part Three
Dependence

Part Four
Independence

Part Five
Interdependence

Part One

Man
and Woman

Chapter 1

The Revolutionary Relationship

Things started off slowly, the liquor had not yet taken effect. The room was somewhat tense and self-conscious, the conversation hesitant. The women noticed a new dress or altered hair style, while the men discussed stocks and complained about the continuing tight money.

It was one of those Friday evening cocktail parties. A dozen couples associated with the Princess Land Development Company had been invited by a prominent architect. Most of the guests arrived late, and each in turn expressed approval of the unusual decor. "I owe it all to Momsy," said the architect. "She runs the house." "Momsy," meanwhile, was giving instruc-

tions to the bartender hired for the occasion and
assisting the guests to get comfortable. The architect
beamed. He looked impeccable in the light blue Eng-
lish-cut suit — which his wife had selected for him.
He chatted amiably with the company president while
his wife assisted the maid in passing out hors d'oeuvres.
She called to him, "Will you get a few more of the tall
glasses from the top shelf, dear?" "Where are they?"
he asked amiably, "I'm not sure I can find them." "I'll
get them myself," she said reprovingly. "He never
knows where anything is." She smiled briefly and
moved officiously to the kitchen, while the architect
continued to talk to the president.

Meanwhile the president's wife, twenty years
younger than her suave, soft-spoken husband with the
ascot and graying temples, was flirting with the handsome personnel manager. The latter was a charming
man in his middle thirties, well aware that the ladies
found him sexy and challenging. He absorbed her with
his eyes while she laughed girlishly at his attentions
and toyed with the buttons on his body shirt: "You
wouldn't know how to handle me." He leered just a
little. "I think I could manage." They had talked like
this before, and soon they moved to the small dance
floor set up in a darkened corner near the bar. The
personnel manager's wife laughed bitterly. "I haven't
danced with him in ten years," she said. "He's got
about as much rhythm as a crocodile. He should dance
with a TV set. He's married to it." The personnel man-

ager overheard and ignored her as he always did.

The president continued talking to the architect. He had noticed his wife flirting with the personnel manager but overlooked her antics as usual. She was his doll; she represented him well, and he could not afford to lose her. This was his third marriage, and he was willing to indulge her extravagance in clothes and jewelry — even in men. He knew that she disliked sex and that her seductive advances to a variety of men were only a part of a game.

The drinks were filled again, and in a different corner of the room the company lawyer and his wife were initiating another one of their famous arguments. "But apartheid works in South Africa," he said. "They don't need half-baked American liberals to tell them how to run their country." They had discussed this many times before. "You're not in the courtroom now, talking to a half-witted jury," she countered. "I know you've always hated blacks. I happen to know something about this issue, and the problem in South Africa is no different from here." Her husband flushed: "Yeh, now that you're able to have lunch with an intelligent black once a month, you're liberated. Maybe you ought to screw a couple of them." "Maybe I already have," she said hotly.

The bookkeeper and his wife had been trapped in the corner with the angry pair and tried without success to calm them down. They themselves never argued; they finished each other's sentences, smoked the same cigarettes, and outdid each other in exaggerated service. "Can I get anyone a drink?" asked the bookkeeper. "Let me get it," said his wife. "No, I will, dear," he insisted. "Try not to put too much liquor in, dear," she said. "I wouldn't want you having another accident like you had after the Christmas party. I was so worried about you." He had not wanted her to bring it up: "That was just a case of slippery pavement, dear," he said. "I know, darling, but the liquor may have dulled your reflexes a bit." "I suppose you're right, dear. I'll go easy on the liquor." His wife turned to the lawyer: "Are you two going away for the holidays?" The lawyer stared coldly at her: "Yeh, we're going to spend a week in the zoo in separate cages."

The senior vice-president was sitting in an easy chair talking to the wounded wife of the personnel manager. He was holding forth on the "stupid ecologists who consider earth movers and dozers ruinous and immoral." As he talked, she kept her eye on the dance floor. The vice-president continued: "They won't be so damn worried about the terrain if they can't pay their rent." His own wife, shy and nervous, had learned long ago not to utter an opinion. She simply nodded in agreement and stood by, making certain that he was comfortable. "There are just too many damn dreamers," he said, spilling his drink. His wife jumped up to get a paper towel in the kitchen. She brushed him off gently as he ignored her completely. He glanced at the president and felt disappointed that he was still chatting with the architect.

He continued to talk: "Everybody wants something for nothing. These young bastards don't know what a day's work is." His wife nodded: "It's even hard to get a cleaning lady," she said. The personnel manager's wife still had her left eye on the dance floor: "It's the mini-skirted bitches that bug me," she said, "And the stupid gigolos that fall for them."

The drinks were filled again, the architect's wife continued to fuss, the lawyer and his wife continued to boil. The voices were louder now and more excited. Laughter echoed through the room, as music sounded and colors flashed. The chemistry had taken effect, and suddenly it was a party. But more than a party, it was a marriage-go-round, a mad carousel of men and women relating to each other in artificial and monotonous roles, reenacted that night in a thousand different places, in a thousand different ways.

Here at a typical cocktail party are revealed the cross dynamics of the marriage-go-round. It is not simply the gathering of husbands and wives, but a collection of men and women leaning on each other, controlling each other, blaming each other in frozen marriages, unable to find the rhythm which could transform their fear and dependency, their anger and weakness into love. Our psychological research utilizing the Pair Attraction Inventory (offered in this book in abridged form and called the "Love Attraction Inventory") has revealed recognizable dynamics in thousands of marriages.

The patterns which our research has revealed are

exemplified in the story of the cocktail party. We
distinguished six such patterns or pair relationships
which characterize the behavior of most couples in
interaction. They are:

(1) The Nurturing Relationship: Mothers and Sons
(2) The Supporting Relationship: Daddies and
    Dolls
(3) The Challenging Relationship: Bitches and
    Nice Guys
(4) The Educating Relationship: Masters and
    Servants
(5) The Confronting Relationship: Hawks
(6) The Accommodating Relationship: Doves

Each of these pair relationships can be exploitative
or manipulative (as those in the cocktail party) or
they can be creative or rhythmic. When a couple
either consciously or unconsciously allows their relationship to freeze or rigidify in any one of these ways
it becomes manipulative. When a couple instead
understands that their relationship can be a continu-
ous workshop for growth, their relationship becomes
actualizing or rhythmic.

In the cocktail party, it is apparent that the architect and his wife have become manipulating mother
and son; the president and his wife manipulate each
other as daddy and doll; the personnel manager and
his wife are bitch and nice guy; the senior vice presi-

dent and his wife are master and servant girl; the lawyer and his wife are hawks; and the bookkeeper and his wife are doves.

These are men and women who are not really relating to each other. They are leaning on each other for survival, or avoiding each other out of fear, or competing with each other — often destructively — out of personal inadequacy. They are reliving the roles they learned in childhood, struggling to grasp from another what was denied in their parents' home, rolling around in a continuing carousel with no end in sight. To fall off is to be alone. To remain on board is to retrace the mad circle till death, always relating to each other in the same way, always playing the same role, reducing creative love to a well-rehearsed part. To stay on board is to fear a relationship.

These six pairs consist of individuals in an immature stage of growth. Extensive research reveals that they have unconsciously exaggerated one part of their personality precisely because they unconsciously denied or repressed another part. In our diagram explaining the dynamics of relationship pairs (see Figure 1) we describe the relating couples according to their capacity to express *strength or weakness* and *anger or love*. These we call the polarities or tensions of interpersonal relating. A rhythmic person can express these polarities with balance. In the manipulative person there is a lack of such balance, so that one of the polar-

Figure 1 THE PAIR RELATIONSHIPS

Adapted from *Man the Manipulator, the Inner Journey from Manipulation to Actualization,* Everett L. Shostrom, Ph.D., Abingdon Press, Nashville and New York, 1967.

ities is exaggerated precisely because the other is denied. When such persons relate, their relationship becomes frozen and rigid.

Four of the pair relationships we have called dependent or complementary because they consist of individuals who are trying to find in their relationship what is missing in themselves. These pairs support the theory that "opposites attract." Thus the master and the bitch have to a greater or lesser degree denied themselves the expression of love. Consequently their anger or control is exaggerated, and they relate in a complementary way to the servant and the nice guy respectively, both of whom express a fawning and manipulative love because they have unconsciously denied their anger. The daddy and mother play the role of strength and unconsciously deny their weakness. They complement and are complemented by the doll and the son, who exaggerate their own weakness and deny their strength.

The remaining two pairs, hawks and doves, we have called independent or symmetrical because they independently fight for control and support the relational theory of "like attracts like." Actually they avoid each other in mutual manipulation. The hawks, in any male-female combination of individuals at the top of the diagram, unconsciously compete with one another because they deny their weakness or love and exaggerate their strength or anger. The doves, in any male-female combination of the individuals at the bottom of the diagram, deny their anger or strength to control each other with weakness or manipulative love.

Obviously no relationship can be precisely identified because each marriage deals with unique human beings whose relationship can never be the same as anyone else's. But we are able to identify patterns of relationships because men and women have been so little able to be themselves. They have sought to end their loneliness and personal pain, their guilt and anxiety, their sadness and insecurity, by asking another to do what each must do for himself or herself. They have been paying homage to the cultural creation of marriage, rather than becoming what they are capable of being. There *are* recognizable patterns in relationships, even if no couple perfectly fits the pattern. Our case studies are actual, with details changed to protect the privacy of our clients. We believe that people will be helped to understand the dynamics of their relationships by the patterns shown in Figure 1. We believe that it is important for a man and woman who marry to understand why they marry a particular person, to have some knowledge of the unconscious pattern of behavior which has determined their choice, and to know what they are really looking for in a marriage. It is important for them to recognize the dependency and immaturity, the rigidity and competitiveness which may have led them to a manipulative relationship and keeps them locked within it. By understanding the patterns of their relationships, men and women can more readily grow towards actualization or rhythm. The average couple contemplating marriage have only an opaque and formless feeling to guide them in making one of life's most vital decisions.

The same "average" couple will often be told by layman and professional alike: "You will know when you are in love. There is no need to ask." This maxim is not true. It is brutally false. Only when one knows what really happens between a man and woman can he distinguish what is the beginning of a love relationship from what is merely the living out of a neurotic illusion. One must know the full range of possible alternatives — which run the gamut from creative fulfillment to dependency and exploitation. The wisdom of choice requires the knowledge of options. To have such options demands that men and women understand the patterns of relationships which psychological research has shown to be present. For this reason our cocktail party carousel merits serious study.

Soon another party was over and the guests had left. But the carousel did not cease to roll. It carried them wherever they went. These were not, however, circus animals locked on a revolving machine. These were men and women locked in a relationship from which they could not seem to escape, a relationship which, indeed, they hardly understood.

Returning to Figure 1, we now may see the cocktail party in a new light. The host and his wife are obviously a mother/son pair. But the host is not really the quiet, docile son he seems to be. He turns his weakness into impotence and denies his own strength. His wife, too, exaggerating her strength, plays a power role and hides her weakness behind her dishes and services, her fussings and pettiness. If each could be rhythmically strong and weak, they could relate in new and exciting ways.

Again looking at Figure 1, it appears that the president and his wife are a daddy/doll pair. They are also confused about srength and weakness. The doll, like the son, transforms her weakness into a manipulative tool. The daddy, on the other hand, much like the mother, displays his strength in a power role and hides his weakness in his fawning indulgence of her seductiveness. Each must learn to express genuine strength and weakness before their relationship can become rhythmic.

The personnel manager and his wife exemplify the bitch/nice guy pairing. They are confused about anger and love. The anger of the bitch is hostile and destructive precisely because she cannot express her tenderness and love. She is a wounded woman, fighting for her life, choosing to badger or annoy manipulatively rather than openly to express her anger. Her husband, feigning niceness, loves in a distorted way because he denies his anger. If each can learn to balance his anger and love, his relationship can grow.

The vice-president and his wife also need not continue in their frozen postures of master and fawning servant girl. Each of them will have to discover, like the bitch and nice guy, how to be rhythmically angry and loving.

The lawyer and his wife are hawks. In exaggerating their anger and strength, they deny their capacity to express genuine weakness and love. In a reverse manner, the bookkeeper and his wife, who are doves, have never learned to express strength and anger. Thus their love and weakness becomes fawning and manipulative. Hawks and doves can become rhythmic in their relationship when they learn balance.

These are all men and women who very much want the same things from life. If they accept loneliness in the place of true love, fantasy in place of reality, and ritualized roles in place of personhood, it is only because they have given up on growth. They do not know what else life has to offer.

No one taught them how to be persons. No one offered them an insight into what their relationship really means. Most likely they will continue to be lonely, afraid to look into themselves, afraid to begin the long journey to maturity. They will merely repeat the mistakes they learned so carefully in childhood. They reflect the tensions and manipulations of their own parents. The personnel manager withdraws like a nice guy to avoid a conflict similar to the one he grew up with as a child, and his wife still knows the rejection she felt at home from her father. The president's wife still struggles to win her father's approval, while her husband still attempts to satisfy an over-protective mother and to ignore the pain of a father who never had time.

Most men and women enter marriage when they are not able to stand alone, when they are frightened and dependent, when they are lonely and insecure. Most make a choice between the ages of eighteen and twenty-five, when they are totally unaware of their reasons. Such individuals are not really in love but are seeking a partial fulfillment through someone else. They ask another to do what they must do themselves. Thus, as Figure 2 shows, they find a temporary wholeness when they come together in marriage or their relationship. When trouble ensues, as they recognize the rigidity of their roles, the process of mutual blaming begins, and each asks the other: "Why aren't you like me?" or "Why aren't you what I want you to be?" Each shifts the responsibility for his own happiness to his partner. Such a relationship becomes fulfilling and rhythmic when the individuals involved accept responsibility for their own behavior, developing that part of themselves which has been unconsciously denied, or modifying the polarity which has been exaggerated. This diagram is actually a paradigm for all immature relationships, even though its application is more obvious in the case of the complementary or dependent relationships.

Even after a first marriage has failed, such individuals remain unprepared and powerless to choose wisely a second time. They will seek a father or mother

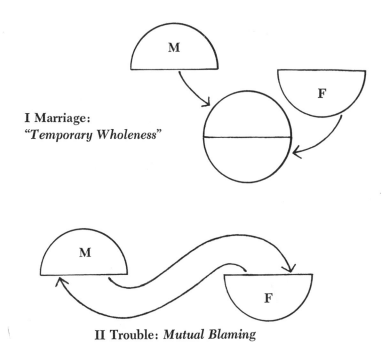

I Marriage:
"Temporary Wholeness"

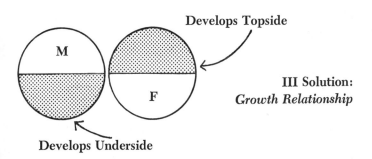

II Trouble: *Mutual Blaming*

Develops Topside

M

F

III Solution:
Growth Relationship

Develops Underside

Figure 2

THE PARTIAL FULFILLMENT THEORY

they never had, still confuse sexual excitement with personal contact, misconstrue service with love, guilt with concern. Often they have only a hazy picture of what marriage can be like. Marriage for them is not an adventure in growth, a relationship between two persons who dare ever more really to be themselves. Instead, it becomes a rigid and deadly dependency, or a fierce and competitive struggle, or even a passive duel between silent adversaries. And often enough, they are doing the best they know how.

Sometimes they are religious and have been taught not to ask much from the present life. The future will provide happiness. They are to carry their cross, raise their children, give of themselves at great personal cost, ignore or repress their feelings, suppress their fantasies and dreams, hide deep within themselves and expect a reward in another, more lasting life. The marriage is final and permanent, they have created their bed and now must lie in it, they have joined the procession of those locked together "until death do us part." And death begins early, much sooner than they expect. So they do the only thing they can: they make the best of it.

Even when they are not religious, they often remain locked on the carousel which only goes in ever-faster circles. When life together has no real meaning, they cling to their children, seek immortality in their jobs, take overweening pride in their homes and possessions, and join the faceless men and women everywhere who have traded their own personal lives for a system.

This is not to say that there are not happy and fulfilled couples in marriage. It is only to say that there are millions of men and women locked in a comfortable arrangement that leaves them lonely and immature. Nor is it to say that the clinging relationship of two dependent people, like that of the bookkeeper and his wife, for example, can never provide any happiness. There are women who will perhaps find some meaning in mothering a man for the whole of a lifetime; and that man will also be content to remain a smiling, helpless son. There are daddies who seem only to want dolls and spend a lifetime with a preening, narcissistic complement to themselves. It is enough for them to show off an exciting package, to display a thing of beauty which seems to give status and power to the possessor. There is the man who finds meaning as the total master of a woman, for whom life is good when he discovers a servant girl who will devote her every motion to his happiness and comfort. Men and women have learned such roles in their childhood homes, in romantic literature and superficial movies, in textbooks which defined men and women in elaborate stereotypes.

But, increasingly, men and women want to be whole persons. They are asking more than roles and stereotypes. They want to be themselves, and if they are to be married, they want to relate as they really are and not as some vague, societal judge insists they must be. Increasingly, the young are suspicious of the carousel. They have seen it at home and it turns them off. They wonder if marriage can work; they wonder if they will not lose their own identity as persons when the luster of novelty and excitement has worn away.

We share their concern. Thus we advocate a changing vision of marriage, a revolution in attitude between man and woman. What we advocate is, in reality, a part of the greater revolution that has taken hold of society. It is the revolution that refuses the limitations put on man by the social institutions he himself has created. It is not merely a revolution to liberate woman from past stereotypes or to free man from the impersonal horror of technology. It is a human revolution to bring men and women back to life.

Most of the problems in psychotherapy have to do with men and women who do not know how to have a creative relationship. Relationships are sick and dying because men and women remain rigidly locked in behavior patterns that forbid rhythm and growth. It is the individuals, the longing, hurting, searching men and women, that need help — not the relationships. They will ultimately be healed not merely by becoming autonomous and independent entities, but by sharing their individual beings, their uniqueness as persons — which they have regained in personal revolution — in a relationship which enriches each, fulfills each, inspires each to a life neither could have alone.

Man is not revolting against marriage because he cannot love deeply and permanently, nor because he does not have the "will to love," but because he refuses to replace love with duty, reality with roles, honesty with acting. He is revolting against a life without surprises, without the chance of growing, without the thrill of discovery. He is revolting not because he has lost his taste for life, but because he sees what life can really be. He is revolting against *death*.

Thus, the marriage institution is under assault in a revolutionary age. Many of the young choose to live together instead of signing a contract which seems often enough to transform a joyous union into a battlefield or a stagnant compromise. Many more, not so young, whose marriages have failed, hesitate to enter marriage again. Young or old, they want to live, to explore, to grow, to leave the carousel with its endless circles of sameness. To them the carousel is death; there is no future, there is nothing but the dull repetition of the past. They will look carefully at marriage, but they will not accept it as it has been previously defined. They are men and women who have begun to abandon absolutes they once considered immovable. Religious and legalistic concepts of marriage will not stand in their way.

This is a book about what can take place between man and woman together when they search for life. This is a book about what marriage *is* and what it can be. It looks at the marriage-go-round and it looks beyond it. It sees the dependency relationships which remain fixated in mutual manipulation. It sees the hostility in pointless competition and the destructive power of passive avoidance. It asserts that in place of such dead and rigid relationships, there can be a revolutionary alternative — which we have called the rhythmic relationship.

The rhythmic relationship is shown in Figure 3. We have simplified the personality by using the same polarities or tensions for the sake of clarity, and our ensuing chapters will deal with each component more elaborately. In the rhythmic relationship there are ideally no denials or exaggerations of the polarities. Each person has his own identity or core, and thus is able to express strength or weakness, anger or love. Each is free to relate as he or she really is. There are no frozen roles. The arrows in the diagram indicate that each person is different at different times, but the entire personality is open and free enough to relate to the partner in a real way. Thus, each can be a variety of things to the other, and nothing in either personality needs denial or distortion. It goes without saying that there are endless degrees of rhythm, and marriage becomes a kind of "workshop for growth." Such couples are not really dependent or independent. We call them interdependent. They are continually in contact and take the risk of expressing their innermost feelings without rehearsal or tailoring. Like two revolving pinwheels, they are constantly "in touch."

There are indeed couples who enjoy such a relationship in greater or lesser degree. We have all known them. They are not stereotypes clinging in fear and

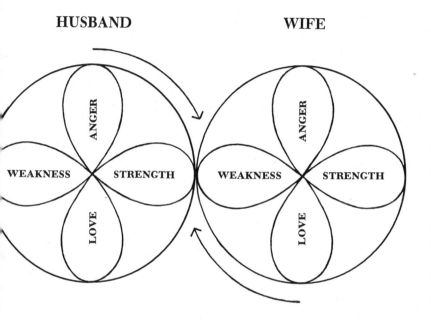

Figure 3

THE RHYTHMIC RELATIONSHIP

dependency to their constricting roles. They are not slashing at each other, holding each other up, leading each other through life. But neither are they rigidly independent. They are men and women who can be a variety of things to each other. At times they can be as a mother or father, a son or daughter to one another, a consoler or confidant. They can be many things. But most of all, they are friends. Each can be himself.

But more than that, we believe that the rhythmic relationship is not simply a protection of personal uniqueness, nor the safeguarding of mutual independence.

The rhythmic relationship is the creation of a new reality, a third substance *(tertium quid),* which neither individual could produce by himself. It is the creation of two strong people growing stronger and together rather than two weak people clinging to each other for life or battling each other in aggressive competition or passive rejection. This is not to deny weakness or need in their relationship. But it is nourishment without absorption, nurturance without the sacrifice of self. It gives meaning to the term "soul mates" who share with one another at ever greater depth and move beyond themselves into a new creation, to become more loving, aware, compassionate, creative, and joyous than they could ever be alone.

Such individuals can relate because they are able to stand in their own uniqueness, to taste their aloneness and solitude as persons, to experience the core of their own being, their personal pain and joy, their sadness and love. They are able to "withdraw into the desert" and to discover there, in isolation, the beauty and strength of themselves. They are able to confront cultural imperatives that have held them prisoner and begin to live for themselves, not for society or its symbols.

They may have found it necessary to seek another kind of job, new friends or a different style of life. Often they have had to come to grips with the seductive slavery of affluence, bring a marriage to an end or a dramatic beginning after years of phoniness, face personal fear and guilt, begin to live for themselves and not for others, cut the umbilical cord sharply and finally, know who they are and not pay homage to what others expect them to be.

Such individuals increasingly begin to have "the courage to be," to recognize how they lost themselves in their parents' home, how their inner self was buried beneath piles of cultural rubbish. They cease blaming their parents, their jobs, their educations, their children, their marriages, their tragedies or astrological signs for their misery and unhappiness. They become responsible for themselves, cease begging approval, and — perhaps for the first time since they gave away their psyche in childhood — begin to know who they are and what they want from life. They perform the most human action of all: they abandon martyrdom and join in the creation of themselves.

Then they begin to be free enough to choose from a

variety of options open to them. These we will consider in this book. We still believe that for most men and women the marriage option is the most satisfying one, that it can be the most fulfilling, the most exciting. But it does not have to be defined as it was in the past. There are no definitions, there are no rules, except the basic ones agreed upon by sound and healthy men, namely the love and concern which make people human. But within the marriage option there are a variety of possibilities, as there are, indeed, in the single option as well. Regardless of the option which men and women choose, the relationship between them is primary and can be unique and sacred. It can indeed be the most creative experience in life, and in reality, such a relationship is what life is all about.

There is great loneliness among men today. The nuclear family of a new age is isolated and often lost. The impersonality of a crowded world only increases the alienation. We are a fragmented people, but even our fragmentation is a sign of hope. Men and women want to be persons, not clichés, not cultural manne-quins. They know they can be. It is our hope that this book will help many to understand their own relation-ships, to know where they are in a relationship, to know why they are there. Above all, it is our hope that more men and women can know the rhythmic relationship that gives life its most important and satisfying meaning.

Perhaps the real tragedy of the cocktail party which

we described at the beginning of this chapter is that the couples involved were not able to see each other as persons. When the president's wife flirted with the personnel manager, she was not looking at him, but only manipulating him to fill momentarily her own emptiness.

The personnel manager's wife looked at her and could not understand her pain. She saw a color pattern, a sexy threat to her marriage. There was no person there. Even the president looked beyond his wife and saw a little girl who offered him stature and success. The lawyer and his wife also avoided each other, struggling unconsciously to prove supremacy because they could not express their need for love and acceptance. The bookkeeper and his wife spent a lifetime backing away from each other in sweetness, lest they experience the pain and joy of closeness and genuine feeling. When the guests were gone, the architect and his wife cleaned up a bit and remained locked in the loneliness of their respective roles.

Suddenly the room was quiet, the glasses empty, the ash trays filled and the coffee table smudged. The laughter born of alcohol and desperation died away. Couples went home together separated by a million miles. No one had been able to extend a hand, to say a word, to hear a voice. They had come as strangers, laughed as strangers, seduced and manipulated as strangers, and left as strangers as well. Nothing had really happened. It was just the marriage-go-round at the circus, the rolling carousel of loneliness. And even the clowns, when they took off their makeup and went to bed, could only stare at the ceiling and wonder what it all meant.

Chapter 2

Male
and Female:
Rigidity or Rhythm

The man-woman relationship centers in sexual differences which the cultural revolution makes increasingly difficult to define. Recent studies indicate that we must replace our comfortable theories of innate constitutional differences between the sexes with the admission of a kind of "psycho-sexual neutrality" at birth. This is not to deny that man is the person with a penis and woman the person with a vagina, nor is it to assert that either organ is likely to be classified in time as vestigial. It is to say that man is capable of fatherhood and woman of motherhood, and to the degree that fatherhood and motherhood are not the prime sexual emphasis in the culture, the accepted differences between the sexes will not hold up. It is further to say that with technological changes which do not require a predominance of physical strength and muscular prowess in daily life, the sexual differences will be increasingly less pronounced. There will be time for men and women to be persons together and not merely roles apart.

Beyond the seeming absolute of man as father and woman as mother, there is little about which the philosophers and feminists, the psychologists and religious prophets can agree. Past definitions of masculinity and femininity have little merit. The Freudian bias, the result of superficial observations and religio-cultural prejudices, can no longer be maintained. Woman is not the penis-hungry, envious, vain, passive and inferior creature that Freud described. Nor can man be satisfied to defend an artificial superiority and strength he does not feel.

Culture, of course, and social institutions have made man and woman vastly different. Man, the aggressive hunter, and woman, the submissive mother, developed attitudes and postures which made their roles definable and acutely distinct. Currently, however, in man's many-sided struggle to be human, the once-accepted categories of sexuality are being abandoned. It is increasingly more important to be a person than to be just male or female — or black or white, Jewish or Christian, American or Russian. Man creates such dogmas and unyielding dualities from his own fear. Now the person, whether male or female, can discover himself in the process of living rather than be defined in the narrowness of cultural imperatives. In the past, the Christian and Jewish God was described as man, the Redeemer was a man, even the generic title for the race is "mankind" or "man." Now it is the person that counts, not in some form of personal narcissism, but in the creative process of self-discovery and honest relationships.

Once, of course, it was very clear what constituted maleness and femaleness because man and woman were largely explained in terms of active motherhood and fatherhood. Psychologists could speak simplistically of man as aggressive, penetrating, and active; woman as receptive, submissive, and passive. Man was the hunter and fighter, woman the mother and nest builder; man the theorist and warrior, woman the healer and peacemaker. The Jungians saw man in terms of the *logos* principle (wisdom, logic) and woman in terms of the *eros* principle (relatedness, feeling). To some, woman was Mother Earth, and man, the father spirit. Man the protector and woman the nourisher. But each authority fell into the trap of attempting to define as "natural" what the culture had created and shaped. Genesis called Eve the helpmate to Adam, St. Paul asked wives to "obey" their husbands, and the Christian marriage ritual incorporated such attitudes in nuptial celebrations. Labor laws, divorce laws, social customs and institutions helped to make such biases sacred and permanent. The "male" and "female" natures were offered as an artist's ideal for every man and woman.

A "feminine" man or "masculine" woman were considered to be tragic distortions, or even perversions.

Such definitions now seem closed and arrogant. Absolute certainty about sexual differences — beyond potential fatherhood and motherhood — are impossible to maintain. Masculinity is what the person capable of fatherhood discovers it to be in the process of living. Femininity is also the personal discovery of the woman capable of motherhood. This is not to sanctify the powerful penis or to glorify the vagina and womb. It is to acknowledge them as functional: the penis is long enough to deposit seed in a place where conception and gestation can take place without invasion and harm.

We are not demeaning culture nor scorning its effects. The cultural attitudes about what is masculine and what is feminine will be with us for a long time. Despite the efforts of the "Zero Population Growth" devotees, motherhood and fatherhood will continue. And despite the changes in child rearing which may come relatively soon, few of us are as yet prepared to abandon what has become a sacred sharing between man and woman: the conception and natural birth of a child.

Neither can we deny the fact that millions of men and women have found great meaning in their roles as father and mother. Cultural decisions, in spite of their fallibility, are not insane. They reflect the times and concerns which fashioned them. But as culture and society change, so does the vision of what it is to be male or female. We are not insisting that man and woman must be something other than they have been. We are saying that they *can* be and unquestionably *will* be. The options are broader, and men and women will no longer be bound by the definitions which froze their relationship into rigid categories. Categories which were born in the culture can die in the culture as well. It is frightened individuals that demand rigid adherence to cultural forms, but it is equally frightened individuals that scorn and reject them utterly.

It is not our cultural heritage that is to be scorned, but the rigidity that refuses to accept new freedom and change. The threat of overpopulation requires us to reassess the large family and the position of the full-time mother. Technological change requires us to re-evaluate the labor force and the place of man and woman in such a force. The rising revolutions to end war and exploitation, to challenge technology and a consumer society, are helping to create a new context of life in which both man and woman can be more open and honestly human. Unquestionably, the biological differences between the person with the penis and the person with the vagina have been reflected in the psyche as well, but such differences need not be locked in the rigid categories of the past.

A refusal to recognize cultural changes and to adjust to them has often left man and woman searching for mythological ways in which to preserve their "masculinity" and "femininity." Thus man the hunter was pressured into becoming man the athlete whether he willed it or not. The narrow-shouldered, sensitive, somewhat passive male was taught by overt and subliminal pressures that he was somehow a failure. The jock-strap became the symbol of manhood in our society. The athlete was said to win the woman, to look the world squarely in the face, to have the right qualities which would insure success in the aggressive world of business. The sporting contest became a kind of life symbol and even the man who was unable to play was expected to be as informed about various teams as a dedicated fan. It was "feminine" to be uninformed or disinterested. Man must be the competitive animal; he must learn to win under pressure, to accept challenges and to struggle for victory no matter the odds. For a time, the Sputnik crisis gave more status to the male intellectual, but the masculine goal then became the mind of an Einstein in Tarzan's frame.

Woman, too, with more leisure time and fewer children, was bombarded with myths. She must search out "feminine" things to do. She must not compete with man, must not put him down, must not enter areas of work or recreation strictly reserved to the male animal. When there were not enough creatively "feminine" things to do, the nest builder was encouraged to become the wily seductress. She must be prepared to handle a man, to conquer him with sexuality, to overpower him with cleverness and charm, to appear weak so that he might be strong. She must flatter him, dress for him, please him, seduce him, disarm him, wait for him, parrot his opinions, avoid arguments, submit to his decisions. Her power would be in her ability to control a man. And man, made artificially strong by her apparent weakness, reinforced this mythology. He insisted that she remain at home, that she devote herself to clothes and kitchens, to the PTA and bridge clubs, that she be protected from the savagery of life. She did not know about "man's world," she had little to contribute to "man's conversation," she was to appear as a child — cheerful, simple, sensitive, frightened — who needed a man to safeguard her from life and her unpredictable impulses. This was the ultimate in mutual manipulation.

Of course, the world of commerce has been on hand to feed the anxiety which created the masculine and feminine myths. The Madison Avenue models have upheld masculinity and femininity to sell their products. Man has been offered a variety of sports and equipment to remain the hunter. His car has become a powerful symbol of his diminished force and independence. His clothes have set him apart as truly aggressive and polished. Professional sports have become big business to win his allegiance. Women have been smothered with fashions and styles, and cosmetology has become a giant industry to help madam keep her male animal intact. Women have been obliged to worry about their figures, their orgasms, their social grace, their homes, their capacity to entertain and to know what a man was talking about. Everywhere there have been lessons and products, magazines and activities, manuals and models.

To preserve such a myth is enervating and expensive. It does not demand that one knows who he is, but that he display an acceptable image, that he play the right role and represent the right cliché. Parents, baptized in the myth, worry about their children. A girl must not display "masculine" tendencies lest she drive men away or become a lesbian. A boy must not throw like a girl, must "get in there and fight," must learn how to compete, must avoid any "homosexual" tendencies or mannerisms. Meanwhile the psychologists have developed their categories of "masculine" and "feminine" by reflecting on the culture, hardly aware that Madison Avenue has been as much a source of their descriptions as any kind of male or female nature created in the culture.

The confusion about masculinity and femininity in a changing world has put tremendous sexual pressures on man and woman as well. With the birth of the pill, sex has been less directed to conception and child bearing; instead its value as a source of pleasure has been emphasized. The size of the penis has been the subject of as great a concern as the duration and frequency of orgasms. To be a man is to be a competent stud, and to be a woman is to attract as much male attention as possible. Pants have grown tighter, skirts shorter, movies and magazines have become more frank and "real." The pressure of sexuality has been everywhere — in the selling of cars, homes, pools, clothes, wigs, after-shave lotion and even tires. The woman who once complained that every man she dated tried to take her to bed is now frequently disappointed if he does not try. The man who comes on strong is frequently depressed and lonely when the sexual experience is over.

Studies have indicated that women enjoy sex as much as men, and other studies note the rise of male impotence under the new demands. The underground press and even the above-ground press have talked of the exciting swingers and the orgies of sexual exchange. Men and women who are not handling a real sexual relationship have fantasized solutions to feelings of personal frustration in such sexual experimentations. More has been demanded of sex than it can give, but the appetite only feeds on the anxiety which keeps men and women off balance. The joy of sexual intercourse has often become the measure of personal success. To be a man is to preserve an erect penis for any kind of action. To be a woman is to satisfy a man with animal fury and the right combination of sexual gyrations. The confusion has continued to grow. Sexual excitation is everywhere, on newsstands, on street corners, under typing tables where mini-skirted thighs tease and promise fulfillment. Such madness and compounded propaganda have demanded a counterattack, and it has come in a variety of revolutionary movements.

The hippies came as a strong and prophetic antidote

to a sexually confused society. They threatened it at its core, with armies of gentle men and women who often dressed alike, looked alike, talked alike, and created a life-style which challenged the mythology of masculine and feminine. The fashion designers would be ready to reproduce the hippie styles in fashionable and expensive reproductions and thus, in the usual American way, to reduce a revolution to a harmless fad. But this time they were only partially successful. The hippie movement has continued, less self-consciously, less addicted to drugs and wandering teenagers, and represents a new style of life which is affecting all of society in quiet and growing ways. But above all, it sees man and woman as persons and brushes away the sexual stereotypes of history. And it has torn away the affluent symbols of a life-style which freezes man and woman in destructive and rigid sexual roles.

The Women's Liberation Movement, with its ancient triumph of feminine suffrage, can perhaps become the most effective revolutionary tool of all to challenge sexual stereotypes and permit women, and men as well, to be persons. Basically, the movement seems intelligent and determined. It fights for equal job opportunity and challenges women to abandon the seductive roles designed by a materialistic society to keep them buying, but keep them little girls and slaves as well. It has helped to liberalize abortion laws, to provide the pill for the unmarried, and to make woman conscious of the need for special education and self-understanding.

It has helped to teach her independence and has torn at the cultural biases which leave her manipulating and helpless.

At times the WLM becomes strident and abrasive. In such thrusts, man naively becomes the enemy. No longer will he chauvinistically dominate women, no longer will he make of her a sexual object. Masturbation will take care of sexual needs, and women will deal only with women until man gives up the place which society has forged for him. Hostilities long-buried and repressed come spewing forth. Unfortunate personal experiences are transformed into general indictments. Angry and frustrated women ask for all-out war and encourage the kind of competition which has done so much to dehumanize man in the business world. These extremists not only demand equal job opportunity but also are determined to surpass man and bring him to subjection, or to avoid him and thus bring him to his knees — his withered penis hanging meekly and uselessly in his once-domineering loins. There is no humor here, no warmth, no compassion, no awareness that man's life has been also rigidified into a form of slavery by the demands of history and culture.

And frightened men, challenged by the strident and aggressive chapters of the WLM, fight back. Extremism begets extremism. The noble goals of the WLM, which are in reality as liberating of men as of women, are lost in the heated conflict. The competitive way, which has so extensively done its damage throughout all societies, tries again to establish love and understanding by manipulation and aggression. Consequently the male extremist, as defensive as his female counterpart, laughs at the women and promises to drive them back to the kitchen. He will rape them with the all-conquering power of his penis. He proclaims the obvious superiority of masculine power, but even as he speaks, one can sense the uncertainty in his inflection and the tension around his upraised chin. The female extremist, attempting to speak for all women from her own unhappiness, denies any difference at all between the sexes. She ignores a cultural heritage, has no respect for the inroads it has made on the feminine character, and seems to overlook the fact that thousands of women have been deeply satisfied with their established roles as wives and mothers. She can only see such women as deluded and victimized, even though they themselves can speak of great personal freedom and demonstrate unique creativity in their life. The extremists can talk of a brave new world in which sexuality will be reduced to a gray neutrality beyond male and female, beyond penis and vagina — despite the fact that numberless men and women have found great joy in their relationships.

But beyond extremism of any variety, we advocate a new and exciting revolution in which men and women will listen to one another and remove the mythological pressure of sexual rigidity, which has only served to make them lonely and confused. We ask that men begin to understand the pain of a woman whose person has been transformed into a sexual object, who has been denied an outlet for her considerable talents, who has been consigned to the home as her only honest domain. But we ask as well that women begin to listen to man as he reveals the pressure of maintaining a strength he doesn't feel, of living in a competitive world which has abused and dehumanized him, of fighting for affluence in place of ego and meaning, of relating to a woman who was childish and petulant, of proving his maleness by his salary and symbols of success because he was not involved in a genuine relationship with his wife. And gradually, in such honest communication, understanding and compassionate, the rigidity of sexual differences is challenged and men and women begin to discover the meaning of their personal sexuality in their new and undefined relationship.

In the wholesome revolutionary context we propose, men and women are not the enemies, but rigidity and dogmatic definitions of masculinity and femininity are. Advertising and media are, as are entrepreneurs and commercial whores who exploit the very confusion of men and women struggling to make life mean something joyful and beautiful. Competition between the sexes only compounds the problem, only extends the illness of a sick society. Such revolutionary men and women are tired of competing, as tired as they are of upholding the artificial roles which society has called masculinity and femininity. Men can acknowledge their weakness, express their feelings, admit their sen-

sitivity, demonstrate their tenderness, reveal the emptiness of their jobs, their power, their symbols of success.
They can expose their fear of women, their need to
control, their refusal to accept criticism, their deep
jealousy and insecurity. Women, too, can recognize the
manipulation in their seductive wiles, their refusal to
deal with men directly, their avoidance of responsibility, their delay in growing up. They can begin to express
their anger, to permit their aggression and power to
come to the surface, to accept their sensuality. They
can admit their boredom, their personal dullness, their
refusal to enter into life with dignity and creative
power. Often they are tired of their roles, their empty
conversations, their inane diversions and social gather-
ings, their inability to trust another woman and to grow
close to her in sisterhood. And the men can admit that
they are tired of Wall Street as well, tired of selling their
souls to business and production, tired of the conversation which centers perennially around affluence and
better deals for making money or better ways of
seducing women. Such men and women are tired of
talking about male and female rights; they are ready
to learn about their rights as persons and to discover
their own sexuality in a relationship which is challenging without being competitive, liberating without denying individual genius. The person is the thing, the
sacred reality, and the existential person will be discovered not in textbooks and seductive commercials,
not in health salons or the manuals of new sexual posi-

tions, but in the creative and exciting opportunity to relate as persons.

But to relate as persons and not as rigid symbols has its own particular pain. It is in many ways easier to live with a rigid and well-defined sexual role. Such a role provides a defense against the pain of becoming human. To live outside such a role is to abandon one's defense, to experience one's personal pain, to relate to another human being with real feeling. Because the pain of growth and change is acute, many people prefer to remain with their cultural role. Neurotically, they attempt to find a variety of symbols to insulate them from the primal pain of childhood — prestige, power, sexual conquests, affluence, and a rigid, definable marriage — but they will live with only occasional moments of satisfaction. The tension brought from childhood, the pain of being manipulated and unloved at home, the truly human pain which must be felt to be dissolved finally — all of these will remain ever-present behind a complex neurotic system of defenses which make friendship and real marriage impossible. To play the cultural role of man or woman becomes increasingly dishonest when the person beneath the role is unreal and unhappy. The role, learned in childhood as a way of satisfying parents and the culture, is an ultimate denial of self. To live in the role is to live with symbols that never satisfy.

In this book, we devote six chapters to marriages which are rigid and neurotic, which lock men and women into roles that often enough seem to make them secure and happy, but which in reality are only the right combination of neurotic dependency. Such marriages must be rigid to survive. When either partner seeks to escape the role which has been defined in the ritualization of courtship and early marriage, the neurotic balance is destroyed. The daddy/doll and master/servant marriages are extreme caricatures of "masculine" and "feminine" roles as defined in past cultures. The selected role helps the man to feel like a man, the woman like a woman — precisely because they do not feel at all, but bury their person in the safe and accepted. The mother/son and bitch/nice guy marriages are, in the traditional sense, a role reversal in which the woman is more "masculine" and the man more "feminine." The reversal may well be the result of the refusal of a man and woman to accept the cultural definitions of sexuality. But such marriages, too, are frightened and rigid — men and women hiding behind their roles rather than discovering themselves. Hawks and doves have a quality of homosexual rigidity about them. The hawks fight like "men," actively and aggressively. The doves fight like "women," passively and gently. In a sense, they are not relating at all, but competing, trying in vain to win the love denied them by a parent.

Beyond such rigidity, we advocate a new *psychology of* persons. Men and women can be persons. They are not seeking in a frozen relationship to fill up some void of childhood which will remain a void unless they experience the pain of growth. Women are not required to abandon the home in order to prove their worth as persons, but are currently freer to explore new roles, to move beyond roles to discover their real selves. Men are not required to lose their aggressiveness and drive, but they are permitted to do so without ceasing to be men. There are no definitions to satisfy in the search for personhood. Men and women are permitted to relate to one another, not by denying the tension and excitement born of sexual differences, but by discovering their sexuality in the very thrust of the relationship. They are not required to be something they do not elect to be. They can be persons first, not role-ridden men or women.

At times a woman can be a kind of mother to her man, at times a child, at times aggressive, strong and active. Similarly the man can be a kind of father or son, he can be gentle, passive, even submissive. Either can cross and recross the sexual lines which culture has established. Each can be a variety of things to the other in the beauty of a friendship between man and woman, with all the rhythm of tension and growth, self-discovery and awareness of the other. Either can be angry or forgiving, sensitive or strong, sad or understanding. There are no rules, no rigid categories, no frozen relationship. There is only the rhythm of life and of persons.

In the rhythmic revolution, we propose that rigidity is the enemy of marriage and human relationships. It is an effort to fit a role rather than to be a person. It is the ultimate manipulation in a marriage wherein each person marries his own manipulation. A partner is asking a partner to become what parents never were, to supply needs that cannot be satisfied, but only symbolically sated for a time. Rigidity is to devote one's self to unreality, to expect what can never be had, to seek health and satisfaction from a source which can only give temporary relief. The rigid person not only remains in his sexual role, but demands that the other remain in a consistent role as well; and the two locked persons reinforce one another in their effort to run away from pain that can never be escaped. The very rigidity of the role is itself the defense behind which the person hides.

There are, indeed, male and female, and the rhythmic tension of their relationship is the source of human life. Such polarity is the very power of life. It is like the tension between germinating seed and soil, between gravity and the resistance to it. The changing seasons are the polarity of life and death, creation and conquest, union and distance, aggression and submission, and in such tension is born beauty and wonder. The light struggles with the darkness and overcomes it only to fall before the splendor of night, only to rise again with the dawn. To be one is to be neutral, to be gray, to be static, unless it be the oneness of life which is alive because it is not content to be the same. Such conflict is creative, such polarity is the substance of growth, such tension is the secret of life.

The polarity and union of male and female is more than the source of biological life and birth. It is not hard to produce children, and as marvelous as is the wonder of childbirth, it ceases to be a miracle in a world which is lavish with life and sudden with death. The true marvel is human love. Sick men and women produce sick and starving children. They seek to find in their children what they never found in themselves and they make of their children empty symbols of their own parental unreality. A man and woman in a real relationship, rhythmic and loving, whose very love is an embracing of a partner as he is, can produce a child capable of love because he has been surrounded by it from birth. If his parents are playing a role, he will know in the beginning that he must play a role as well to win their love. And even as he plays it, perhaps successfully and completely, he will also know that the love will never really come. The love is not for him in his reality, it is for him in his neurotic emptiness.

Even the homosexual often seeks to create the tension of male and female in his relationships, but seldom seems to succeed in his battle with nature's profound determination of what is man and what is woman. Perhaps if society is more accepting of the homosexual — as it must be — his journey will not be as painful as it has been. He will have greater opportunities to understand his homosexuality rather than simply fight society's blind bias. He will not have to proselytize for his own security and assert that the goal of society is to

reduce the polarity of the sexes to some homosexual
sameness with artificial psychic tensions. This is as
unrewarding as the role-playing of man and woman.
The homosexual will probably not find lost parental
love in a partner who is equally as deprived and
wounded He will find it only in passing through the
pain which leads to personhood and the celebration of
his own self as worthwhile and beloved. Only then can
he truly decide whether or not his homosexuality is
culturally derived. Meanwhile, he should have the same
right as any other person to pursue life in honesty and
openness, and not be persecuted by cultural stereotypes
which reflect our ignorance and prejudice.

It is impossible for anyone to know how man and
woman will develop, but we do not believe that creative intercourse will give way to some laboratory of
conception and childbirth. Nor do we believe that
parthenogenesis will destroy the institution of marriage.
We believe that the rhythm of the male-female relationship, moved beyond cultural definitions, will only
make the union of man and woman more creative and
loving. Even as there are male and female, they are not
defined or definable. They are persons, unique and
special, together but forever alone, different and challenging. They are male and female, relating with the
ever-changing tension of the sexes, to become what
they are. A man or woman can seek out the partner who
makes growth and response a free and loving experi-

ence. It is the context of such a human relationship of persons that life becomes a fulfilling job. There is no need to search for life's meaning, because it is contained in the very experience of living. Here there is no abrasive competition between the sexes, but the rhythm of discovery and freedom which transforms the polarity of the relationship not into a distant dualism but into a creative dialectic.

As man and woman live together and join in the sexual union, it well may be that woman is softer, man more aggressive, he more like the trees and the sky, she more like the breeze and the grass; but it will not *have* to be. It well may be her softness that makes his penis hard and penetrating, his strength that makes her vagina moist and penetrable. Or it may be her strength that leads him to union, his softness that stirs her. But in any case, it is the rhythm of their bodies in motion that brings each of them to the orgasm which unites them as man and woman. And the unity achieved in this sexual experience, both real and symbolic, is the union of man and woman who have joined together to be more really what they are as individuals.

Here is a relationship between two people who choose to relate, who were not driven by their special neurosis, a relationship between two persons, one male, one female, who search out their own sexuality and another's in the tension of a relationship. And in their union, the tension explodes to include another, and for a time tension disappears in the oneness of their orgasm. They moved beyond sexuality "to be two in one flesh." The tension is gone, the tension which brought them together. And when the tension is gone, they celebrate their oneness in quiet contentment. The tension will return, not the tension of desperation, stereotype and seductive manipulation, but the tension of persons opening to one another, hearing one another, listening to one another, revealing themselves to one another. And in their coming together is the very force of love that permits them to go apart and be themselves. There are no boundaries, no clear-cut roles, no precise definitions, no repressions of self as unworthy and sexually destructive.

In such a context, sexuality is a special way of caring. It is exploration, concern, knowledge, compassion, union. It delights in a penis which can penetrate a vagina without wanting to destroy it, a vagina which can hold a penis without wanting to smash it or take it away. It delights in coming together and consents to move apart as persons. It delights in the rhythmic union of man and woman which is the very source of human creativity and life. It delights in love.

This love is best described as rhythmic. It is not rigid. It can be dependent without leaning, it can be independent without being isolated and arrogantly autonomous. Its very dependence and independence are rhythmic, that is, are aware of another person with whom one comes together and goes apart. Such love is more easily experienced than defined. Such love is the most important element in the relationship between man and woman.

To describe a rhythmic dependence — which is not fawning, smothering, and manipulative, but liberating — and a rhythmic independence — which is not patronizing, aloof, and superhuman, but freeing — we have selected the term interdependence. Such interdependence is the kind of love which transports a man and woman beyond the very boundaries of their own persons in a relationship and, as it were, creates a new reality, a third dimension, a *tertium quid*. Suddenly "the whole is really more than the sum of its parts."

It is a man and woman in love, two persons who in their unconditional acceptance of the being of each other, become co-creators. It is this very acceptance which produces the growth and change which could never be demanded. To demand it is to destroy it, because the very demand is a denial of what already is and a negation of faith in what can be. This is the paradox of rhythmic or actualizing love — that it is created in the very affirmation which refuses to expect or demand it.

Between man and woman — rhythmic and interdependent in their love — there is a new creation, the *tertium quid,* which lifts the being of each to a level unattainable by one's self alone, and again, paradoxically, it is produced by a process which is not effortful. The very determination to try inhibits success. The more effort involved, the more likely a failure.

Rather, it is the excitement of two beings in harmony which creates the new symphony of becoming. A relationship which is a "workshop for growth" unites play with work in an exciting adventure.

Perhaps no one to our satisfaction has said this better than an attractive young woman who had recently escaped the domination of a rigid husband who demanded change. A professional man, he attempted to create her in his own image and in the process lost her to another man who offered her the freedom to be. Suddenly an angry concept of a relationship became a flowing perception. "We just flow together," she said, "somehow we just evolve. I can't describe it, but I know that I am more myself each time we are together — and more than myself. His very being seems to make me blossom. I don't have to work at it. It just happens. We are open to each other — naked and unashamed."

This is the new creation of love, the so-called leap of faith, faith to cherish and accept what already is in order to create what otherwise could never be.

But there is no creation — no new reality — if woman becomes like the man whom she permits to hold her a prisoner. Nor is anything gained if the insecure man rises up to conquer the woman who has resented her role as passive and submissive spouse. It is in the rhythm of discovery and freedom that man and woman unite. Neither can create life alone, neither alone can nourish it or take credit for it. It is the mystery of their union which reproduces the creative mystery of all of nature. Where men and women fear to be different, they will not come together; where they fear to be the same, they will not go apart. They will not be persons, they will not know the liberating joy of a man and woman bound in closeness, of two persons who have moved beyond the rigidity of death and fear to the rhythm of life and joy. They will know manipulation, control, posturing, need, dependency, role-playing, but never the rhythmic freedom of a man and woman in love.

In ancient mythology, very often the origins of human life came from the mysterious marital union of earth and sky. Maybe this says it best of all. It is impossible to choose between earth and sky, to know who is master and who is servant. But in the union of the heavens and the earth, there is an end to loneliness and rigidity; there is wholeness, completeness, and the rhythmic, life-creating union of man and woman as persons.

Chapter 3

Marriage and Divorce: Options, Old and New

Paul and Irene were married shortly after the Korean conflict and had four children in seven years. Paul completed college during the early years of marriage and took a job developing tract housing projects. He worked long hours, made increasingly good money, and drifted away from his wife and children. At first Irene had shared the excitement of his challenging job, but gradually she resented the many evenings alone. She was tied to the children, had given up her education, traveled only occasionally with Paul, and distrusted his extracurricular activities. She did not like her jealousy but felt increasingly that she had grown too "housewifey" to keep Paul interested. Her temper flared frequently at the children.

Paul did not expect much of Irene. Occasionally he wanted meals and sex, someone to take care of his clothes and phone calls, someone to discipline the children and to entertain at home once or twice a month. He was generous, never questioned her charge accounts, and even encouraged her to buy fashionable clothes. Actually the marriage had ended emotionally soon after it began. There had never been much real communication, and although Paul was insecure in his competitive job, he could not talk to Irene of his pain and fear. Only the symptoms of his tension appeared — moodiness and excessive drinking, outbursts of temper and restlessness. He had lost the humor and softness of his college years and had engaged in a series of abortive affairs, but had never really thought of terminating the marriage.

Nor did Irene think of divorce, even though she knew that the marriage was superficial and unreal. She wept frequently, got behind in housework, and listlessly watched television or read in the evenings. When Paul finally arrived home, he mixed a drink, talked excitedly of his business deals, or sulked quietly about his problems. He never seemed to hear Irene, content that she had a nice home, her own sports car, a pool, a country club, and a secure future for the children. Irene knew, despite her disappointment, that she was married for life. She could only look forward to the day when the struggle would be over and together they would know once again the fun of their courtship.

It was after twelve years of marriage that Irene finally went to her pastor for help. She had to talk to someone. Her crying spells were frequent, she screamed regularly at the children, and arguments with Paul were loud and hysterical. The pastor was her only recourse since she trusted him, and Paul could not ignore his suggestions.

The pastor listened sympathetically to Irene's complaints. She was well-regarded in the parish, as was Paul. They had supported a variety of programs and gave generously to the church. The pastor encouraged Irene to be more understanding of Paul's work and admonished Paul to give more time to his family. He suggested that they spend some time together away from the children. But a two-week vacation in Acapulco only made them realize how little they had in common.

They were, however, trapped. The church insisted that their marriage was sacred and permanent, and even though divorce was possible, it was an admission of radical weakness and personal failure. Their social milieu upheld the church's attitude. There was really nothing to do but to endure. The pastor had not helped them, professional marriage-counseling was suspect, and therapy was an admission of mental illness. Meanwhile growing children needed attention and Paul's work made increasing demands.

Irene had developed symptoms of an unhappy marriage: headaches and back aches, frequent colds and arthritis, menstrual pains and the inability to sleep.

Paul could more easily act out the signs of his unhappiness in his job. There were secretaries to flatter him, partners to applaud his success, expense accounts to keep his mind away from himself. In reality he did not ask much from marriage and saw no reason to end it. Irene represented him well. Divorce would not look good on his record. It suggested a man who was not able to keep his affairs in order. No one was disturbed about occasional alliances with women or even a mistress as long as such dalliances were not public and messy. They were almost expected of a virile man. But Irene was needed to create the right image and to provide him with the kind of domestic roots that gave stability to his life. He did not need a relationship; he was not ready for one. But he feared divorce. Aside from business reasons, divorce meant an incredible expense, and Paul was not prepared to jeopardize the affluence which was his greatest defense against personal insecurity. The divorce laws, like the laws of the church, were designed to keep marriages intact.

It was not only the pastor who made it difficult for Irene to think of divorce. It was her parents as well. Her mother, subdued by Paul's effusive charm, often told her how lucky she was to have a man who could give her everything. Her father, who had known only the economic slavery of the factory, bragged continually about his successful son-in-law. In their minds there would never be a reason for divorce or even separation. Paul did not beat her, he was not an alcoholic, nor did he abuse the children. Irene had a greater share of the American dream than did her parents and had, therefore, no reason to complain. It did not matter that Paul shut her out of his life and treated her as an indentured servant with buying privileges.

Paul had made a few concessions after the counseling experience with the pastor. He took Irene to lunch occasionally, made several expensive purchases, encouraged her to take art lessons, and raved about her talents. Irene recognized his fear of divorce and used it to get more of his time and more expensive clothes. But the clothes only had superficial meaning, and increased time with Paul meant more emptiness and ritualized reactions. She poured her frustrations into the children, yearning for their love and attention, setting herself up continually for a variety of rejections. She spent more time at church and in programs of social service, constantly sought someone's approval, and occasionally permitted herself to enjoy the attention of strange men. Her symptoms of loneliness only increased. She made more visits to doctors, fought with the children, quarreled with friends, and gained weight. She began to fantasize sexual experiences with other men; her dreams became erratic and disturbing, and finally, after a "nervous breakdown," she sought professional help.

After almost a year of therapy, Irene was able to recognize that she wanted a separation from Paul. When the separation proved ineffectual, Irene was free enough to file for divorce. She had broken the hold which the church had on her, the chains which her parents had molded almost from birth, her dependency upon Paul and the comfortable way of life he provided. She had remained a child, asking from Paul what she could never receive, fantasizing her pains away. She had blamed her parents, the church, Paul's job, the other women in his life, and, of course, the children. Finally she broke with Paul and her past and began to be responsible for herself.

At first, Paul was relieved by the separation and divorce. He dated frequently and lived with a few women for brief periods of time, but soon became weary of the plastic scene. He began to drink heavily, lost time at work, could not tolerate being alone, became deeply jealous of Irene, and began to trail her whenever she left the house in the evening. Finally, he sought help and began the painful process of self-discovery. Gradually he realized that he was an emotional child who got up every day to prove that he was worthy of someone's love and went to bed every night not believing it. He was two people — one a successful businessman who stood outside and looked in at the other, a lonely little boy who only felt his own emptiness. There was no center to his personality, but only an endless conflict between the boy who wanted love and the man who tried hopelessly to earn it by his accomplishments.

Paul and Irene, like millions of other couples, are victims of a rigid cultural system of marriage and divorce. They cling to a marriage long after it has disintegrated because they fear to escape. They learn that a marriage contract is sacred and permanent, that divorce is a crime, that they must hang on to satisfy society's demands. Often enough, the marriage contract is a trap; it leaves a couple guilty and passive; it is rigid and artificial. It asks for commitment at a time when it cannot honestly be given. It can only be freely offered when time and experience make it unnecessary. And even though theoretically a divorce is possible, the couple who attempt it are usually made to feel selfish and sinful. In reality, contracts are not sacred at all. Fidelity to a marriage contract has no meaning since love cannot be legislated. The very notion of a marriage contract represents a distrust of the persons involved and is an expression of society's fear of men and women. The contract makes marriage a rigid institution rather than a rhythmic relationship.

The churches, too, have helped to rigidify marriage by institutionalizing Christ and reducing his spirit to a frozen system. Christ's simple message of man's love for man as the authentic expression of his love for God was reduced to dogmas and rules. In the marriage contract, the churches transformed a vision of love into the coldness of a permanent obligation. Couples have exchanged everlasting vows long before they have known what a relationship is all about. They have pledged fidelity when fidelity has no significance unless it comes from the spontaneous joy of a rhythmic relationship. Legislated fidelity does nothing to strengthen love or to make it grow. Thus, marriage becomes an unyielding framework where love is expected and even demanded, rather than a free environment where creative and permanent love is made possible. No one can honestly vow permanent love. He can only promise present willingness to try. Only men and women afraid to love need the childish security of a binding contract. And when the love dissolves or time establishes that love is not present, then the same childish fear moves a man and woman to act out their tantrums in an angry and vengeful divorce.

Nor does it matter how empty a relationship has become or how destructive of human feeling it really is. Orthodox and rigid Christians can still call it a "sacramental union in Christ" as long as two baptized persons have exchanged vows. It is only important to satisfy the demands of ecclesiastical laws whose origin is lost in history. A rigid and unhappy relationship is called the will of God. Often enough the very Christian sacrament is the instrument that encourages the playing of a role and makes rhythmic love impossible. Men and women, bound in guilt and mutual destruction, are encouraged to pay token respect, to suffer and wait, to manipulate and expect "God" to do what they must do themselves. Ultimately, such behavior becomes a denial of personal responsibility, and the contract is worth more than the man.

The world of commerce has ever been on hand to

make a profit from the rigidity of the marital contract. The "sacred" ceremony has become a lucrative business. An elaborate and costly celebration, loudly supported by the culture, has helped to put additional pressure on the man and woman involved. Couples are encouraged to buy and wear expensive rings to symbolize the beauty and permanence of their love before they know what marriage is about. Church weddings, gowns, attendants, receptions, music, and floral arrangements surround the ritual with tinsel and artifice, and increase the pressure. The bride and groom, vulnerable and anxious, are the unwitting victims. Soon they will be pushed into mortgages and insurance programs, annuities and life-styles, car and furniture payments — long before they know if they have the basis for a growing relationship. And when love and affection are lacking, the attendant guilt ensues. Men buy homes they cannot afford when they are spending too much time away from their families. Then they spend even more time away and develop intense financial pressures to perpetuate the life-style which their guilt created. Women, sensing that they are losing their husbands to business, increase their wardrobes, pour money into beauty aids, worry about their figures and orgasms, fight the advancing years — all in attentive response to the commercial suggestions for recreating a disappearing love. The entrepreneurs are ever ready to feed the neurotic fear and guilt which lie at the roots of millions of marriages.

In the past, there have been few options available to

men and women who begin a relationship. Living together without marriage has been considered immoral. Marriages are expected to last for life. In such a social and religious milieu, most men and women marry in their early twenties, have children almost immediately, succcumb to the male and female stereotypes, and move into their well-defined and separate worlds. They ask little from each other as persons except that they keep the rigid rules established for husbands and wives. For a couple of years or less, they enjoy each other, and then they settle into the pointless routine of marriage, looking forward to the day when life can mean something more than routine responsibility. When that day comes, they often discover that they have nothing to share but memories and dullness.

It has not been considered important in the contractual marriage that men and women grow. Marriage has not been an unconditional acceptance of one another, but a rigid fulfillment of a contract. Husbands must know their duties, and wives must fulfill their obligations. It is not even important that they become close. It is enough that they cling, that they control one another, that they compromise their deepest feelings, that they "get along," that they live through each other in a kind of childish dependency. This still represents a fulfillment of the marriage contract and an endorsement of the sacred vows. Often such couples call their marriage happy, glancing at each other nervously, hardly aware that they have lost touch with their feelings, recognizing that they must be happy because life offers them nothing else, or because a "happy" marriage is often enough the gauge of personal worth. They married because they were not able to live any longer alone, and they remained married because they have signed a contract and do not know what else to do. The man is content if his wife is satisfied, she is content if he is. This is, of course, not a description of some few marriages which are truly fulfilling and creative. It is only a description of millions which somehow endure. And a rigid and puritanical society is happy that such relationships do not become the statistics of rising divorce rates. They fulfill the contract.

It is essential, however, that such couples remain faithful. This means that the partners should not sleep with anyone except each other. Emotionally they can be miles apart, but adultery is a violation of the contract and grounds for divorce, except in the most rigid circles. A woman may well be emotionally closer to any number of men than to her husband — her doctor, her art teacher, her pastor — but if she goes to bed with anyone else, the sacred contract is violated. Sexual intercourse is the gauge of sacramental fidelity.

The Marriage Option

As we have affirmed, we still believe that for most of us, the marriage option is the most satisfying and that it can be the most fulfilling and exciting. We also believe, however, that the rhythmic relationship does not come effortlessly and that the majority of us learn by our sincere mistakes. Today there are afforded us a variety of options in our journey to establish a rhythmic relationship, and the experience of these options well may contribute to growth.

The Divorce Option

When a couple recognizes that their marriage is pointless and unhappy, there is the divorce option which is usually as rigid and unreal as the marriage contract itself. For Catholics and devout Protestants or Jews, the divorce option has been difficult to assume. Even though a divorce is permitted in most religious sects (and even among Catholics a number of theologians recognize the dishonesty of the traditional position on divorce and remarriage), the stigma of divorce is hard to endure. Divorce often means severing one's ties with one's family and a deep wounding of one's self-image. There is the fear that children will be traumatized, there is the hurt to parents, and there is the hostile legal system which helps to make unhappy spouses bitter adversaries. The divorce laws, despite their modest improvement in some areas, are often rigid and unyielding, and they attempt to punish the unworthy woman and especially the unworthy man who failed. In the cultural stereotype, man is likely to blame, wandering animal that he is, and he must pay accordingly. He has used a helpless woman, burdened her with his children, neglected his marriage, and upset the common weal. Often it is almost impossible for a man to begin a new life because of the intolerable financial burdens. Most lawyers, too, hedge when one talks about fees and attempt to extract what the traffic will bear for their clerical duties — a kind of symbolic slap at the rigid law by its legal defenders.

Of course, there are other pressures as well. The man and woman have to consider their reputation. There are all of the social clichés which contain so much of the religious bias and legal vindictiveness: "If one marriage fails, how can another succeed?" or "Divorced women are 'free and loose,'" or "The children will become delinquent." There are the defensive individuals who know that their own marriage is threatened by the dissolution of one close to them, and they are ready to protect their own shaky kingdom at any cost, even by vicious gossip and painful attacks.

The Separation Option

Under the pressures and traditional rigidity of the marriage and divorce code, many men and women hold out in a meaningless marriage. The marriage option has been unsatisfactory, but it seems better than the divorce option. Often enough, the *separation option* without the help of lawyers would be worthwhile and liberating.We call this a "creative separation," and the conditions for the separation are agreed upon by the couple in the presence of their counselor or therapist. Normally, the man moves out and takes his own apartment. During the first several weeks of the separation, we encourage them not to communicate at all. The process is explained to the children where it is feasible. This gives individuals a chance to evaluate themselves independently of the pressures of a relationship. Divorce is as rigid and as final as the marriage, and even though a divorce can frequently lead to a new and meaningful relationship with someone else, equally as often the unhappy couple can make a serious effort at reconciliation through separation and professional help. Normally, after about six months the couple will be able to begin their marriage — or end it.

Unhappiness in marriage is frequently enough the result of emerging unconscious negative feelings which did not arise in courtship or were blocked for a variety of reasons. But the rigidity of divorce does not consider the positive forces which brought a couple together originally and which still may exist. Such forces can make a genuine marriage possible if a couple has time to work out their individual differences in a "creative separation" with skillful professional help — to work on one's self rather than on the relationship. Increasingly, it is recognized that a great number of *interpersonal* marital difficulties are a projection of one's *personal* frustrations and pain onto a spouse. It is not unusual for an unhappy and deeply insecure person to create circumstances whereby divorce becomes inevitable.

He or she refuses to accept another's love because of a deep rejection of self.

The individual who deeply rejects his own being must learn that his rejection of another is merely a reflection of his own lack of self-love. Such a person needs personal therapeutic help before he can enter a creative relationship. He can merely manipulate, project, and neurotically depend. A relationship would only be painful and disastrous, or superficial and unreal. No amount of "work" will salvage it. A man and woman must be ready to build a relationship. A relationship can only be as mature as those who enter it.

Frequently marriage counseling has been as biased as the churches and society and as hurtful as the lawyers and the courts. Many counselors have seen themselves as saviors of a marriage, and in their inability to deal with two separate individuals apart from a relationship, they have merely compounded the problem by offering facile communication techniques which provide temporary assuagement. Often true feelings of hostility are only more deeply repressed, and the beginning of hope becomes a deeper despair when the relationship breaks down again. Numerous individuals, now divorced and remarried to someone else, still have a deep attachment for their original spouse. Often, early in marriage, they projected their personal problems onto a partner, expecting a husband or wife to make up for the defects of a mother or father. When they moved beyond such rigidity and immaturity to a new self-knowledge, the angry divorce, with all of its pharisaic rigidity, had already taken place. It is paradoxical that the very rigidity of the marriage and divorce options, stereotyped and unyielding, have destroyed many relationships that through the separation option could well have survived and grown fruitful.

The Continental Option

Many couples who remain in unhappy marriages select one of the few other options that are available. They become absorbed in their work and go their separate ways, communicating only at the most superficial level. A large number, however, exercise the *continental option* in which the couple remain married but look to other relationships to satisfy sexual and personal needs. The continental option has been widespread in countries where rigorous religious laws forbidding divorce were absorbed into the law of the land. But it also has been widespread in America where puritanical rigidity makes divorce difficult and unsatisfactory. Most of us know many people who exercise the continental option; most of them are men, although an increasing number of women are also exercising this option. Sometimes such affairs are long-lasting and satisfying. A wife is maintained to provide a family, domestic roots, and a respectable image. A mistress is kept to provide for sexual and emotional needs. The more immature prefer the continental option — with a variety of partners. And the continental option has become increasingly more acceptable. Increasingly women too have been able to avail themselves of this option, disturbing the myth that woman is more monogamous by nature.

Woman is unquestionably more monogamous by culture than man — man has seen to that. Because he is more exposed to the world generally, his sexual potency seems to be more frequently threatened. Woman has played along with the myth, rejecting "infidelity" as unworthy of her "motherhood," or insisting that man's sexual needs are more urgent. Often her mouthing of the myth has been a ploy to keep her man faithful when he is "out in the world." If she is obviously faithful, then it will be more difficult for him to be unfaithful. In reality, men and women are capable of being "faithful" when a relationship is real and satisfying, when sexual appetites are not a means of dealing with neurotic needs. But either one is capable of being "continental."

Sex in our society has become a great outlet for the neurotic to deal with personal anxiety, depression, and a feeling of being unloved. Many professionals have seen sex problems as the key difficulty in the man-woman relationship, rather than as a symptom of a deeper personal and relational defect. Paradoxically, the very rigidity of the sexual taboos in society have increased the importance of sex and have asked it to resolve problems that it cannot touch. Many couples have sex far more frequently than they really want —

as a means to handle personal anxiety. Extramarital affairs, similarly, are often a search for something that another sexual alliance will not give. We believe, too, that the cultural prophets who speak of a future world in which the sexual act will take place almost as simply as a handshake between men and women are asking sex to provide more than it can and are denying its true meaning in the context of a close and mature relationship. The tension between persons seeking closeness is often dissipated and lost when it is transferred to a sexual dimension, rather than being pursued and explored in a verbal way. Often enough the "word" is lost in sexual communication. Innately, however, it cannot be said that either man or woman is more prone to the continental option and extramarital affairs. The continental option, which often is the way selected by men and women who are not free enough to escape a marriage or to enter into it, is usually only a temporary relief — a way of dealing with the symptoms of personal pain rather than reaching the core of such pain which lies deep within one's self.

The Exchange Option

Among the partially liberated people, there are new and dramatic experiments which also look to sex for personal liberation. Such, for example, is the *exchange option* in which sexual partners are shared. Sometimes such experiments seem to give new meaning to a dead and routine sex life between married partners. More often they create jealousy, confusion, loneliness, depression, and lead to divorce. Such artificial liberation is again asking sex to do what it cannot ultimately do. It is asking sexual variety to heal a sick and wounded soul. A variety of sex can unquestionably distract a man or woman from the personal pain and emptiness of a marriage or a life. It will unquestionably create greater sexual stimulation where routine intercourse has been effete and dull. But it will not reach the core of personal need, nor touch the spirit of man which eludes sexual solutions. In reality it is another way, often a very rigid one, of leaving a man or woman as insecure and searching as before. Ultimately it may well take away from sex altogether the excitement and stimulation that it provides.

The Fantasy Option

Most unhappy men and women who are locked in their meaningless marriages live with the *fantasy option*. It is cheaper and often safer than the exchange option, takes less time, and permits an endless variety of partners without risk. Those who live with the fantasy option are content to masturbate with regularity and imagination, often using pornography to assist them in their creative imaginings. They go to movies which offer them sexual outlets. *Playboy* tells them what they have missed or are missing in the affluent society. Miniskirts and tight pants are everywhere to feed their fantasies. Normally they do not do anything about this plethora of sex except dream and masturbate. But their private world does offer them temporary respite from personal pain and dullness, loneliness and boredom. Many of the religious orthodoxies and puritan traditions have made of masturbation a moral problem. Some have called it a "mortal sin," or have named it "self-abuse." Others have observed that it will weaken the mind or impair the health. Tragically, the churches and moral prophets did not sense the real problem which lay beneath the life of sexual fantasy, the personal pain and loneliness — which, indeed, deserves the concern of us all. The fantasy option is not often a happy one, and often those who exercise it are guilty and depressed. Perhaps they flirt, tease surreptitiously, anticipate the day when they will be free from their dull and binding relationship, build up increasing sexual tension without satisfying outlets, and often end in impotence and frigidity in the only valid sexual contact permitted them. Sex becomes the wandering savior who comes to deliver them from the prison of their own misery.

Very often when an unhappy couple have moved beyond the intermediate options to divorce, the severance comes years after it should have. The divorce is often not painful and vituperative at all, but anti-climactic. The couple has paid their guilty dues to God and society by lingering in a dead union. They attempt to face the guilt imposed by parents and friends, by divorce laws and eager lawyers; and in loneliness they must begin again. Usually they are not prepared for

the single life and often could not take the final step
until they knew that a partner was waiting for them
after the divorce. If there is no waiting partner, it is
hard to begin another life. Women can derive emotional
support from the children and the home, sometimes at
great cost to the children, but they are bound by the
home and children as well. If the children are grown,
women are often uniquely lonely and unprepared to
work in a world they abandoned years before. They are
not prepared for the uncertainty and pressure of dating.
Often they take what they can get and marry again or
live alone as martyrs endowed with alimony. Divorced
men, too, find it difficult. Many seem incapable of living
alone. The very insecurity which has driven them at
work and led to an accumulation of ego symbols pre-
vents them from being alone. They are prone to enter
another marriage which may well soon become as
chaotic and unsatisfying as the first. They still have
not dealt with the primal pain which lies at the root of
their own personality, and another marriage may only
produce a rearrangement of their neurotic needs. The
divorce option, when it finally comes, with all of its
rigidity and rancor, is often as unsatisfying as the
alternatives.

The Living-Together Option

The new freedom between the sexes, which modern
life provides, offers a variety of new options in the
relationship between man and woman. The widespread

lifting of the taboo of premarital sex does not push couples as readily into marriage as a means of obtaining sex on a regular and satisfying basis. Most men and women are able to have a variety of sexual experiences before they enter marriage. Young couples, and some not so young, choose to *live together* for some time before they consider marriage, or agree to live together as long as they want without marriage. Thus they avoid the pressures of contractual marriage and the rigors of a vituperative divorce. Some consider the first years of their marriage as a pre-parental option during which they adjust to one another before they have children. Some couples join with others in the communal option, with or without the exchange of partners in sexual inter-course. Many couples decide not to have children, and if the marriage breaks up, the woman refuses to accept alimony because she considers it a patronizing gesture to her womanhood.

We are not suggesting that all of these options actu-ally create greater personal freedom and more satisfy-ing relationships. Sexual experience, no matter how extensive, does not necessarily assist in personal matur-ity. It depends on the honesty and reality of the sharing. It well can be the perpetuation of a hangup. And couples who live together without marriage often dis-cover that the cultural stereotype of husband and wife are as much a part of their relationship as it would be if they had signed a binding contract. There is the same rigidity, the same role-playing, the same effort to find in a spouse what was denied by a parent. And despite the great freedom between the sexes, insecure men and women are still entering marriages for manipulative reasons, fearing that they might lose their partners if they are not bound by a contract. In many places, the new sexual freedom is mere talk, and the same inhibitions that troubled the parents now plague their children. And millions of men and women, young and old, want marriage because they believe in it and hope to know the joy of a deep and satisfying relationship.

We, too, believe in marriage, although we believe as well that the greater freedom and honesty of our times make possible more fulfilling alliances between man and woman. It is not God who truly holds a couple together, not a contract, not children, not manipulation or rigid role-playing. What holds the couple together is the freedom of the partners to be persons in rhythmic relationship. Increasingly, this is what the men and women of today are asking. In reality, that freedom was always possible; it was only more difficult to challenge the rigidity of religious myths, cultural stereotypes, and contractual definitions. It was hard to oppose society and tradition. It is easier now to resist artificial life-styles of affluence which only serve to separate a husband and wife and their children. It is easier to deal with the guilt imposed by parents or social structures. It is easier to be honest about one's real feelings. The humanistic revolution of our times has made it possible. We are not naïve enough to think that the battle against rigidity is won, but the relationship we propose will make it easier.

The Growth Option

We believe men and women must grow individually and together. They can accept the fact that a deep and lasting relationship is difficult to come by, that it requires personal honesty and pain and, often, individual professional help. They can more readily discover that the rigidity of past options usually represented an unwillingness on the part of men and women to be responsible for their own behavior. Most of the problems that occurred in marriage were problems that each individual brought to marriage and attempted to solve by controlling or leaning on his or her partner. Now they can more easily recognize, in the light of modern social and psychological awareness, that personal and individual growth is the greatest contribution that anyone can make to a relationship. It is individuals, capable of loving and being loved, who can truly build a marriage. Their marriage will not absorb their individuality, nor destroy their individual goals, nor push them into artificial roles. They will know that only by being themselves can they relate to each other. The alternative is rigidity and role-playing.

In the next two sections of the book, we describe the six pair relationships that our research has revealed most frequently develop between a man and a woman.

It is possible and necessary to move beyond such rigidity to have a real marriage. We have called these static relationships: mother/son, daddy/doll, bitch/nice guy, master/servant, hawks, and doves. Most individuals, who are still fixed in an immature level of growth will find their own relationship described in one or more of these chapters. But hopefully, they will find greater freedom and flexibility to grow in their relationships. In a final section of the book, we will discuss ways of improving marital rhythm and of stimulating greater personal and interpersonal growth.

We do not believe that the marital institution is dying; we only believe that rigidity is. Actually, rigidity is death. Binding contracts and cultural imperatives encourage rigidity, death, and manipulation. The rising divorce rate can well mean not that our world is plunged into hedonism and irresponsibility, but that man and woman are asking a great deal from their relationship. They are no longer satisfied with the rigid role-playing that makes of marriage a permanent kind of dependency or a masochistic endurance contest, and that makes of divorce a vituperative and hostile act of revenge.

Increasingly, man and woman will live together because they *choose* to do so. They will not be bound by contracts and outdated religious codes; they will not be made guilty and anxious by lawyers and priests, by patronizing friends and controlling parents. They will not wait for an eternal life in some vaulted heaven where martyrdom will be rewarded. Life is now, today, this moment.

In the new world of increased freedom, there will of course be impulsiveness and immaturity, as man seeks to lift the weight of the ages off his back. At times his experiments will be rash and futile, self-conscious and foolish. This is the way of the rhythmic revolution which is seeking to find itself and to liberate man. There will be attempts at communal living that will perhaps fail, sexual freedom that will only imprison, efforts at greater communication that will be frustrated. But there will be, as well, a consistent challenge to the emptiness of affluence, the rigidity of the churches, the marital stereotypes of the culture. Some marriages will endure, some will never take place, many will be temporary steps along the way. But the relationship of man and woman will become a creative growth experience. Today, perhaps as never before, in the fortunate lands where life can be lived, man and woman have a unique opportunity to move from the rigidity of the past to the exciting option of a rhythmic relationship.

Part Two

Love Attraction
Inventory

Part Two

Love Attraction
Inventory

Before you begin reading Part II of this book, the
following inventory, the *Abridged Love Attraction
Inventory,* male and female forms, is presented for
your interest and help in making Parts III through V
more meaningful. It is not necessary, but if you and
your "significant other," male or female, take the inventory now, you can compare your individual per-
ceptions about what attracts you to each other. Even
if you take it alone, it will enhance your reading.
When you have scored the inventories and understand
the interpretations (which follow), you can then read
Parts III through V with greater involvement. It takes
only fifteen to twenty minutes.

NOTE: This is not a professional standardized test. If you are interested in more accurate scores, consult a professionally qualified person who can obtain from the Educational and Industrial Testing Service, Box 7234, San Diego, 92107, the full-length, standardized PAIR ATTRACTION INVENTORY *with appropriate normative data which can be administered to you and interpreted by that professional.*

Abridged Love Attraction Inventory
INSTRUCTIONS: MALE FORM

1 Complete the information at the top of your Answer Sheet first.

2 This inventory consists of a number of statements describing your feelings and reactions towards a "significant other" of the opposite sex. Read each statement and mark it either TRUE or FALSE as applied to this person.

You are to make your answers directly on the answer sheet, as is shown in the example at the right. If the statement is TRUE *or* MOSTLY TRUE *as applied to this other person, blacken the lines in the column headed* T. *(See example 1 at right.) If the statement is* FALSE *or* NOT USUALLY TRUE, *as applied to this person, then blacken between the lines in the column headed* F. *(See example 2 at right.)*

Section of Answer
Column
Correctly Marked

	T	F			T	F
1	▉	┊┊	29		▉	┊┊
2	┊┊	▉	30		▉	┊┊

3 Special Instructions: Read these items in pairs, as for example, items 1 and 2, items 3 and 4, etc. Then answer each independently. Reading them together will enable you to describe the relationship in greater depth. Sometimes both in the pair will be true, sometimes both will be false, and sometimes one will be true and other false.

4 Be sure to answer all items. Leave no items blank. Too many blank items will invalidate yor results. Work as fast as you can, giving your first impression. Don't think too long on any item. There is no time limit.

5 In marking your answers on the answer sheet, be sure the number of the statement agrees with the number on the answer sheet.
   Now begin the Inventory starting with Question 1.

Abridged Love Attraction Inventory: Male Form

1 When things get tough I turn to her for help.

2 She always comes through when I need her.

3 I think I like her best when she acts weak and helpless.

4 She likes to act weak and helpless so that I will feel protective of her.

5 I would rather give in than fight with her.

6 She has to be right in practically everything.

7 I have a greater accumulation of knowledge than she.

8 She recognizes my greater knowledge.

9 Sex can be a powerful weapon and I would not hesitate to use it.

10 She will withhold sex if it gains her an advantage.

11 I would rather give in than fight.

12 She would rather give in than fight.

13 She seems to feel that I am continually growing.

14 I feel that she is continually growing.

15 When it is at all possible I always seek counsel from her.

16 She gives me good advice.

17 I greatly enjoy attending to her and taking care of all of her needs.

18 She likes for me to be responsible for taking care of her.

19 I am afraid of what she might do.

20 She will not hesitate to use the threat of a violent or irresponsible act to get her way.

21 When I ask her to do something, I feel that she should do it.

22 She does what I ask her to do.

23 I try to outwit her when I can.

24 She thinks that she can outwit me.

25 I do anything I can to keep peace and quiet.

26 She likes peace and quiet.

27 She is everything I want in a woman.

28 She seems to feel that I am everything she wants in a man.

29 I trust her decisions in important matters.

30 She accepts responsibility in times of crisis.

31 I like to give her presents.

32 She expresses an almost childlike delight when I bring her presents.

33 When she is angry I find it best just to sit and take it.

34 Sometimes she really tells me off.

35 I do not want her to do things without my approval.

36 She would not make an important decision without consulting me first.

37 I like to keep the upper hand in my relationship with her.

38 She struggles to keep the upper hand in her relationship with me.

39 I very much dislike fighting and arguing.

40 She very much dislikes fighting and arguing.

41 I feel free to express my love for her.

42 She expresses her love freely to me.

43 I feel that she is stronger than I.

44 She knows that she is the stronger of the two of us.

45 I quite often see her as a child who needs adult guidance.

46 She looks to me for parental-like guidance.

47 It is easier to let her be boss than to fight with her.

48 She likes to be boss.

49 I want her to be available when I need her.

50 She lets me know that I can count on her availability.

51 I frequently point out to her where she is wrong.

52 She likes to find something wrong with what I do.

53 I like for her to make decisions.

54 She likes for me to make decisions.

55 I know her likes and dislikes.

56 She knows my likes and dislikes.

57 I would not want to make an important decision without her approval.

58 She feels that she is more knowledgeable than I.

59 She tries to make me feel sexually dominant.

60 She is responsive to my sexual advances.

61 I am constantly trying to do things to please her.

62 She never seems to be satisfied with the things I do for her.

63 I expect her to respond to me sexually when I want her.

64 She knows that she should be ready to satisfy my sexual needs.

65 I feel that I can do things better than she can.

66 She feels that she can do things better than I can.

67 I avoid issues that might cause conflict.

68 She avoids issues that might cause conflict.

69 I enjoy helping her on her projects.

70 She enjoys helping me on my projects.

71 I feel submissive in her presence.

72 She is the more dominant of the two of us.

73 I like for her to submit to my demands.

74 She seems to want to submit to my demands.

75 I often take the blame for things in order to avoid trouble.

76 She likes to blame me for things.

77 I am more experienced in the ways of the world.

78 She relies on my greater experience and better judgment.

79 She brings out a contrary streak in me.

80 I seem to stimulate her to argument.

81 I like for her to say what she wants us to do.

82 She likes for me to decide what we should do.

83 I seem to feel what she feels.

84 She seems to feel what I feel.

85 I don't blame her for not trusting me in some things.

86 She doesn't trust me to take care of myself.

87 I feel very protective when I am with her.

88 She feels safe and secure when I am around.

89 I suffer a lot of abuse from her.

90 Sometimes I think she gets a real pleasure out of seeing me suffer.

91 I like for her to be servile and attentive to my needs.

92 She does what I ask without complaint.

93 I feel that I am constantly in competition with her.

94 She feels very competitive towards me.

95 I do not mind if she takes over.

96 She encourages me to take the lead.

97 I seem able to do the things that make her happy.

98 She is a constant source of delight to me.

99 I do not object to her exercising a great deal of control over my actions.

100 She is good at controlling me so that I do what she wants.

101 I like to take her out and show her off.

102 She likes to dress up and go places where she can be shown off.

103 I am often confused as to what she really wants from me.

104 She demands that I be more of a man with her and then puts me down when I try to be.

105 I make the decisions for both of us.

106 She makes only the decisions that I let her make.

107 I refuse to give into her when I know she is wrong.

108 She hates to admit it when she is wrong.

109 If it were a choice of who was sexually satisfied I would rather it would be her.

110 She seems to be more concerned with my sexual pleasure than with her own.

111 My feelings for her grow stronger the longer we are together.

112 Her love for me seems to grow stronger as time goes on.

Answer Sheet for Abridged Love Attraction Inventory:
Male Form

	T F		T F		T F		T F	
1		29		57		85		A1
2		30		58		86		A2
3		31		59		87		B1
4		32		60		88		B2
5		33		61		89		C1
6		34		62		90		C2
7		35		63		91		D1
8		36		64		92		D2
9		37		65		93		E1
10		38		66		94		E2
11		39		67		95		F1
12		40		68		96		F2
13		41		69		97		G1
14		42		70		98		G2

Totals

A1 _____
A2 _____
A3 _____
A4 _____
TOTAL A _____

B1 _____
B2 _____
B3 _____
B4 _____
TOTAL B _____

C1 _____
C2 _____
C3 _____
C4 _____
TOTAL C _____

	T F		T F		T F		T F	
15	¦¦ ¦¦	43	¦¦ ¦¦	71	¦¦ ¦¦	99	¦¦ ¦¦	A3
16	¦¦ ¦¦	44	¦¦ ¦¦	72	¦¦ ¦¦	100	¦¦ ¦¦	A4
17	¦¦ ¦¦	45	¦¦ ¦¦	73	¦¦ ¦¦	101	¦¦ ¦¦	B3
18	¦¦ ¦¦	46	¦¦ ¦¦	74	¦¦ ¦¦	102	¦¦ ¦¦	B4
19	¦¦ ¦¦	47	¦¦ ¦¦	75	¦¦ ¦¦	103	¦¦ ¦¦	C3
20	¦¦ ¦¦	48	¦¦ ¦¦	76	¦¦ ¦¦	104	¦¦ ¦¦	C4
21	¦¦ ¦¦	49	¦¦ ¦¦	77	¦¦ ¦¦	105	¦¦ ¦¦	D3
22	¦¦ ¦¦	50	¦¦ ¦¦	78	¦¦ ¦¦	106	¦¦ ¦¦	D4
23	¦¦ ¦¦	51	¦¦ ¦¦	79	¦¦ ¦¦	107	¦¦ ¦¦	E3
24	¦¦ ¦¦	52	¦¦ ¦¦	80	¦¦ ¦¦	108	¦¦ ¦¦	E4
25	¦¦ ¦¦	53	¦¦ ¦¦	81	¦¦ ¦¦	109	¦¦ ¦¦	F3
26	¦¦ ¦¦	54	¦¦ ¦¦	82	¦¦ ¦¦	110	¦¦ ¦¦	F4
27	¦¦ ¦¦	55	¦¦ ¦¦	83	¦¦ ¦¦	111	¦¦ ¦¦	G3
28	¦¦ ¦¦	56	¦¦ ¦¦	84	¦¦ ¦¦	112	¦¦ ¦¦	G4

D1 _____
D2 _____
D3 _____
D4 _____
TOTAL D _____

E1 _____
E2 _____
E3 _____
E4 _____
TOTAL E _____

F1 _____
F2 _____
F3 _____
F4 _____
TOTAL F _____

G1 _____
G2 _____
G3 _____
G4 _____
TOTAL G _____

Your Name_____

Your "Significant Other"_____

Abridged Love Attraction Inventory
INSTRUCTIONS: FEMALE FORM

1 Complete the information at the top of your Answer Sheet first.

2 This inventory consists of a number of statements describing your feelings and reactions towards a "significant other" of the opposite sex. Read each statement and mark it either TRUE or FALSE as applied to this person.

You are to make your answers directly on the answer sheet, as is shown in the example at the right. If the statement is TRUE or MOSTLY TRUE as applied to this other person, blacken the lines in the column headed T. (See example 1 at right.) If the statement is FALSE or NOT USUALLY TRUE, as applied to this person, then blacken between the lines in the column headed F. (See example 2 at right.)

Section of Answer Column Correctly Marked

	T F		T F
1	▉ ⁝⁝	29	▉ ⁝⁝
2	⁝⁝ ▉	30	▉ ⁝⁝

3 Special Instructions: Read these items in pairs, as for example, items 1 and 2, items 3 and 4, etc. Then answer each independently. Reading them together will enable you to describe the relationship in greater depth. Sometimes both in the pair will be true, sometimes both will be false, and sometimes one will be true and other false.

4 Be sure to answer all items. Leave no items blank. Too many blank items will invalidate yor results. Work

as fast as you can, giving your first impression. Don't think too long on any item. There is no time limit.

5 In marking your answers on the answer sheet, be sure the number of the statement agrees with the number on the answer sheet.

Now begin the Inventory starting with Question 1.

Abridged Love Attraction Inventory: Female Form

1 When things get tough he turns to me for help.

2 I always come through when he needs me.

3 I think he likes me best when I act weak and helpless.

4 I like to act weak and helpless so that he will feel protective of me.

5 He would rather give in than fight with me.

6 I have to be right in practically everything.

7 He has a greater accumulation of knowledge than I.

8 I recognize his greater knowledge.

9 Sex can be a powerful weapon and he would not hesitate to use it.

10 I will withhold sex if it gains me an advantage.

11 He would rather give in than fight.

12 I would rather give in than fight.

13 He seems to feel that I am continually growing.

14 I feel that he is continually growing.

15 When it is at all possible he always seeks counsel from me.

16 I give him good advice.

17 He greatly enjoys attending to me and taking care of all of my needs.

18 I like for him to be responsible for taking care of me.

19 He is afraid of what I might do.

20 I will not hesitate to use the threat of a violent or irresponsible act to get my way.

21 When he asks me to do something he feels that I should do it.

22 I do what he asks me to do.

23 He tries to outwit me when he can.

24 I think that I can outwit him.

25 He does anything he can to keep peace and quiet.

26 I like peace and quiet.

27 He is everything I want in a man.

28 He seems to feel that I am everything he wants in a woman.

29 He trusts my decisions in important matters.

30 I accept responsibility in times of crisis.

31 He likes to give me presents.

32 I express an almost childlike delight when he brings me presents.

33 When I am angry he finds it best just to sit and take it.

34 Sometimes I really tell him off.

35 He does not want me to do things without his approval.

36 I would not make an important decision without consulting him first.

37 He likes to keep the upper hand in his relationship with me.

38 I struggle to keep the upper hand in my relationship with him.

39 He very much dislikes fighting and arguing.

40 I very much dislike fighting and arguing.

41 He feels free to express his love for me.

42 I express my love freely to him.

43 He feels that I am stronger than he is.

44 I know that I am the stronger of the two of us.

45 He quite often sees me as a child who needs adult guidance.

46 I look to him for parental-like guidance.

47 He finds it easier to let me be boss than to fight with me.

48 I like to be boss.

49 He wants me to be available when he needs me.

50 I let him know that he can count on my availability.

51 He frequently points out to me where I am wrong.

52 I like to find something wrong with what he does.

53 He likes for me to make decisions.

54 I like for him to make decisions.

55 He knows my likes and dislikes.

56 I know his likes and dislikes.

57 He would not want to make an important decision without my approval.

58 I feel that I am more knowledgeable than he is.

59 I try to make him feel sexually dominant.

60 I am responsive to his sexual advances.

61 He is constantly trying to do things to please me.

62 I never seem to be satisfied with the things he does for me.

63 He expects me to respond to him sexually when he wants me.

64 I know that I should be ready to satisfy his sexual needs.

65 He feels that he can do things better than I can.

66 I feel that I can do things better than he can.

67 He avoids issues that might cause conflict.

68 I avoid issues that might cause conflict.

69 He enjoys helping me on my projects.

70 I enjoy helping him on his projects.

71 He feels submissive in my presence.

72 I am the more dominant of the two of us.

73 He likes for me to submit to his demands.

74 I seem to want to submit to his demands.

75 He often takes the blame for things in order to avoid trouble.

76 I like to blame him for things.

77 I am more experienced in the ways of the world.

78 I rely on his greater experience and better judgment.

79 He brings out a contrary streak in me.

80 I seem to stimulate him to argument.

81 He likes for me to say what I want us to do.

82 I like for him to decide what we should do.

83 He seems to feel what I feel.

84 I seem to feel what he feels.

85 He doesn't blame me for not trusting him in some things.

86 I don't trust him to take care of himself.

87 He feels very protective when he is with me.

88 I feel safe and secure when he is around.

89 He suffers a lot of abuse from me.

90 Sometimes he thinks I get a real pleasure out of seeing him suffer.

91 He likes for me to be servile and attentive to his needs.

92 I do what he asks without complaint.

93 He feels that he is constantly in competition with me.

94 I feel very competitive towards him.

95 He does not mind if I take over.

96 I encourage him to take the lead.

97 He seems able to do the things that make me happy.

98 He is a constant source of delight to me.

99 He does not object to my exercising a great deal of control over his actions.

100 I am good at controlling him so that he does what I want.

101 He likes to take me out and show me off.

102 I like to dress up and go places where I can be shown off.

103 He is often confused as to what I really want from him.

104 I demand that he be more of a man with me and then put him down when he tries to be.

105 He makes the decisions for both of us.

106 I make only the decisions that he lets me make.

107 He refuses to give in to me when he knows I am wrong.

108 I hate to admit it when I am wrong.

109 If it were a choice of who was sexually satisfied he would rather it would be me.

110 I seem to be more concerned with his sexual pleasure than with my own.

111 His feelings for me grow stronger the longer we are together.

112 My love for him seems to grow stronger as time goes on.

Answer Sheet for Abridged Love Attraction Inventory: Female Form

T F	T F	T F	T F	
1	29	57	85	A1
2	30	58	86	A2
3	31	59	87	B1
4	32	60	88	B2
5	33	61	89	C1
6	34	62	90	C2
7	35	63	91	D1
8	36	64	92	D2
9	37	65	93	E1
10	38	66	94	E2
11	39	67	95	F1
12	40	68	96	F2
13	41	69	97	G1
14	42	70	98	G2

Totals

A1 _____
A2 _____
A3 _____
A4 _____
TOTAL A _____

B1 _____
B2 _____
B3 _____
B4 _____
TOTAL B _____

C1 _____
C2 _____
C3 _____
C4 _____
TOTAL C _____

	T	F		T	F		T	F		T	F	
15	¦¦	¦¦	43	¦¦	¦¦	71	¦¦	¦¦	99	¦¦	¦¦	A3
16	¦¦	¦¦	44	¦¦	¦¦	72	¦¦	¦¦	100	¦¦	¦¦	A4
17	¦¦	¦¦	45	¦¦	¦¦	73	¦¦	¦¦	101	¦¦	¦¦	B3
18	¦¦	¦¦	46	¦¦	¦¦	74	¦¦	¦¦	102	¦¦	¦¦	B4
19	¦¦	¦¦	47	¦¦	¦¦	75	¦¦	¦¦	103	¦¦	¦¦	C3
20	¦¦	¦¦	48	¦¦	¦¦	76	¦¦	¦¦	104	¦¦	¦¦	C4
21	¦¦	¦¦	49	¦¦	¦¦	77	¦¦	¦¦	105	¦¦	¦¦	D3
22	¦¦	¦¦	50	¦¦	¦¦	78	¦¦	¦¦	106	¦¦	¦¦	D4
23	¦¦	¦¦	51	¦¦	¦¦	79	¦¦	¦¦	107	¦¦	¦¦	E3
24	¦¦	¦¦	52	¦¦	¦¦	80	¦¦	¦¦	108	¦¦	¦¦	E4
25	¦¦	¦¦	53	¦¦	¦¦	81	¦¦	¦¦	109	¦¦	¦¦	F3
26	¦¦	¦¦	54	¦¦	¦¦	82	¦¦	¦¦	110	¦¦	¦¦	F4
27	¦¦	¦¦	55	¦¦	¦¦	83	¦¦	¦¦	111	¦¦	¦¦	G3
28	¦¦	¦¦	56	¦¦	¦¦	84	¦¦	¦¦	112	¦¦	¦¦	G4

D1 _____
D2 _____
D3
D4 _____
TOTAL D _____

E1 _____
E2
E3 _____
E4 _____
TOTAL E _____

F1 _____
F2
F3
F4 _____
TOTAL F _____

G1 _____
G2 _____
G3 _____
G4 _____
TOTAL G _____

Your Name_____

Your "Significant Other"_____

Scoring

When you have finished the inventory, get your totals by counting only the TRUES (T's) on each line *horizontally*. Notice that Line 1 are A1 scores, Line 2 are A2 scores, Line 15 are A3 scores and Line 16 are A4 scores. The total of these four lines gives you your A score.

In the same way, count only the TRUES (T's) for "B." Line 3 *horizontally* are B1 scores, Line 4 are B2 scores, Line 17 are B3 scores, and Line 18 are B4 scores. The total of these four lines gives you your B score.

All scores, A-G, are found in the same way as above. Record all totals in the right hand column.

Interpretation

Now compare your scores with Figure 1 on page 22.

Notice that your "A" score is your score for the MOTHER/SON pair.

Your "B" score is your score for the DADDY/DOLL pair.

Your "C" score is your score for the BITCH/NICE GUY pair.

Your "D" score is your score for the MASTER/SERVANT pair.

Your "E" score is your score for the HAWK pair.

Your "F" score is your score for the DOVE pair.

Your "G" score is for the RHYTHMIC pair.

In general, the higher your score, the more you and your "significant other" have a relationship like that of the pairs mentioned above. The lower your scores the less you and your "significant other" have a relationship like that of the pairs mentioned above.

Each of the above pairs has a chapter which follows, wherein the pair is described in detail. You can analyze your relationship in further detail with the aid of that chapter material.

REMEMBER:

This is an abbreviated form of the *Pair Attraction Inventory*. It is not presented as a standardized psychological test. No norms or clinical interpretations are offered. You should understand that it is only for your interest and enjoyment. A score you make one time would not necessarily be the score you would make another time.

If you are interested in pursuing the matter, you should consult a professionally qualified person who can obtain from the Educational and Industrial Testing Service the full-length, standardized *Pair Attraction Inventory* with appropriate normative data which can be administered to you and interpreted by that professional.

Part Three

Dependence

Chapter 4

The Nurturing Relationship: Mothers and Sons

Most marriages are unhappy compromises. They reflect the dependency needs of individuals and have little to do with free and mature choice. The mother/son-ing relationship is perhaps the most obvious. It permits a man to remain a child and to behave much as he did at home while growing up. It permits a woman simply to imitate the role that her own mother played and requires no creative adjustment to mature adulthood. As shown in Figure 1, in this relationship the *weak* son-like husband has chosen unconsciously his opposite, the *strong* mother-like woman. This unconscious choice is suggested in the writings of Freud.

Ken and Yvonne have a typical mother/son relationship. They have been married twenty-seven years and would have remained "well-adjusted" if Yvonne had not become involved with another man. It was strange how it happened. When the three children were grown up and on their own, she found herself with time on her hands. She took a part-time office job as typist and filing clerk for a small construction office. Her boss, Dave, not only liked her efficiency but also seemed to enjoy talking to her. She felt uncomfortable in his presence at first because he looked directly at her when he talked. Occasionally he would put his hand on her shoulder when he asked her about office business, and sometimes he would let his fingers play with her neck. Yvonne never protested. On one occasion, when they were in the office alone, he confronted her as she moved away from the filing cabinet and took her in his arms. He looked directly into her eyes and when Yvonne began to protest, he kissed her firmly and passionately.

"Something inside of me just melted," she confided to me. "I was helpless, it was as if I had never known a man before. I felt my whole body tremble. I had heard all the expressions of the love songs, but I never knew what they were talking about. Suddenly, with Dave, I was helpless and I loved it. He didn't ask my permission, he assumed it, and that very afternoon, we made love.

"I could not believe it was happening. I had never behaved this way before. I had never been unfaithful

to Ken nor really thought about another man. Then
. . . suddenly, there I was, tearing at Dave like an
animal . . . And I liked it. I wasn't ashamed. It seemed
the way it should be.

Gradually she began seeing more of Dave. She made
excuses to be gone for a weekend, had lunch with him
frequently, met him in bars and motels, and permitted
him in her home when Ken was traveling. Ken never
suspected; he even chided Yvonne for working so
hard. Finally she had to tell him. He did not explode,
he merely turned his head away and looked sad. Tears
filled his eyes. He said that he would not talk about
it; he insisted that he loved her, that he needed her,
that he couldn't live without her.

When they appeared for therapy, Yvonne was dis-
traught and apparently frightened. Ken was quiet and
sad. He was handsome, tall and well-built in a delicate
way. His hair was gray and wavy, his face lean and
almost athletic. For thirty years he had held the same
job as an outstanding salesman for a chemical company. He had fought briefly in the war. He dressed
well, in bright clothes, and stood out in a crowd.
Friends considered him the ideal husband. He had
given Yvonne immense freedom.

She had selected their homes and neighborhoods,
planned the vacations, bought Ken's clothes, even
picked out his car. She made the decisions for the children, and fought the family battles. When an electric
can-opener was defective, she called the dealer. When
he resisted, she wrote to the company and received

immediate satisfaction. Ken loved to tell of this to friends. "Mom gets the job done," he said proudly. She cooked well, managed the house scrupulously, budgeted carefully, and planned for retirement. Her energy seemed boundless. Ken and the children were her whole life.

When Ken was asked about their sex life, he said it was "very good." He never initiated sex himself, at the most he would caress Yvonne's arm gently when they were in bed. If she responded slightly, he felt emboldened to touch her breast or to stroke her leg. If there were the least resistance, or even a lack of interest on her part, he patted her arm gently and went to sleep. He realized that "she works hard and having three children is a difficult job." Life was comfortable for Ken. There were no decisions to make, his job was routine and lucrative, the customers had become long-time acquaintances and the competition was not significant. Occasionally he had new ideas for his job, but saw no need to rock the boat. He seemed to enjoy life as it was. He was very understanding of Yvonne's affair even though his eyes filled with tears whenever we talked about it. "I guess she had to do it," he said, "She never should have gone to work. She just wasn't ready for the business world."

Yvonne was an attractive woman. For years she had worn her hair pulled tightly against the back of her head. She was careless about her dress, her glasses did not always fit her properly, she had gained a little weight, and, indeed, she looked *motherly*. When she began to get interested in Dave, her appearance improved unbelievably. She became warm and sensual, alive and passionate. She was in love with Dave and wanted to marry him, or at least to live with him. She had never felt like this before. "My whole being," she said, "comes alive when he's around.

"I didn't really know what sex was. I married Ken right out of college. I didn't finish and he was a senior. I was delighted to have my own home, to have someone who needed me and someone to care for. I had my own kitchen, rooms to decorate, and Ken was always patient and kind. He never complained . . . I knew nothing of sex and what we had seemed satisfactory."

In reality, it was only on the surface that Ken was satisfied. His own mother had babied him, had made decisions continually for him. When he stopped talking about Yvonne and began talking about his early life at home, it was quite obvious that he was hardly aware of the difference between Yvonne and his mother. Some simple psychological exercises were tried in which he became a very small boy again and told his mother that he wanted to play football with the other children. He was asked to act his own part from one chair and then move to another chair and play the part of his mother. When he described how she looked and what she was wearing, it was not difficult to picture the once-dowdy Yvonne. Gradually he got into the spirit of the game and with encouragement began to talk back to his mother. After a long period of time, he began to raise his voice. Asked how old he was at this precise moment, he said: "About fifteen." "Where are you?" the therapist asked. "In the kitchen."

He described the surroundings, what she was wearing, what he was wearing, how each of them looked. As he began to talk, the tears flowed and his intense anger could be felt as he bit out the words. Soon he was shouting at her and sobbing like an adolescent boy: "Damn it. You never . . . you never . . . let me do anything. ANYTHING. Don't do this Kenny, don't ride in the car with Joey. Don't stay out late. Don't drink. Don't smoke. Well, fuck you, Fuck You, FUCK YOU, YOU OLD BITCH. I CAN DO THINGS. I DON'T NEED YOU. GET THE HELL OUT OF MY LIFE!" At this point, Ken fell down on the floor, slapping at the pillow in the chair that represented his mother. Gradually, as he collected himself, his whole expression changed. There was a new fiber in his face, a new determination in his eyes.

Over the next several weeks he began to talk more freely about his feelings for Yvonne. At the therapist's suggestion, they had separated. He had taken his own apartment and was beginning to enjoy it. She was living at home and seeing Dave regularly. It was suggested that they stay away from lawyers and just get the feeling of a separation. Ken had never made any decisions for himself, since he had never been required to. It was not a coincidence that he had selected Yvonne to be a mother to him. It was exactly what he wanted. He married the woman with whom he was ready to relate. At times his resentment came pouring out. He was not even ready to look at Yvonne. She had been lost to him in the stored-up rage he had for his mother. He wanted to visit his mother who was still living in the family home and in good health. The therapist did not interfere with his plans; there was no way that he could have prevented him.

The meeting was a successful one. First he had to tell her of his anger and the way she had treated him as a child and young man. He had been surprised to see that she was actually afraid of his anger and directness. Suddenly a fierce and domineering ogre became a stuttering woman who wanted his love. For the first time in his life he was able to talk to her and to hold her in his arms because he wanted to. She told him about her own marriage, her loneliness, her unhappiness, and he was able to see her as a person. More important, he was able to forgive her for what she had done to him and to have the kind of mother that he had always wanted.

When he returned after the visit to his mother, he was ecstatic. He was able to understand his marriage. No longer concerned about Yvonne and Dave, he ceased wondering about her whereabouts and began to live more fully his new life. He was able to confront his boss with many of his own resentments about his work, was given a young assistant to do much of the leg work and had new courage to seek new and more exciting accounts. He didn't need anyone's permission to act. He was dating a much younger woman who found him extremely attractive, and when he began falling into his boyish patterns of behavior again, as he frequently did, he was often able to recognize it. He began to realize that he did have preferences, interests, opinions, even biases. He had never expressed, nor even tried to express them.

Meanwhile Yvonne continued to find a new happiness with Dave. She wasn't concerned with the neighbors when Dave stayed overnight. She began to realize that she had a life to live that would never return. She was honest with the children and discovered that they were largely willing to take her as she was. A year later she married Dave and made no financial demands on Ken. Ken, too, later married, and found a beginning happiness which he had not thought possible.

Our research reveals that in rigid mother/son relationships, the attraction is not based on love but rather comes from early dependency patterns in the life of each.

The woman assumes the role of "heavy" in the relationship because she learned early in life that this was the way to gain love and attention. In the case cited, Yvonne's relationship with her father which had helped to make her "mother-like." Ken, on the other hand, had an active and driving mother to whom he subordinated himself. His own father was passive and accepted his wife's role as leader in the family.

Marriage locks couples into the mother/son relationship permanently and fixes the dependency patterns, unless some catastrophic experience (such as Dave) occurs to challenge the relationship. Often the couple, because of their unconscious needs, have not explored the field of eligible relationships widely. They are frequently driven to relationships which reflect their past needs and have no picture of the wide range of alternatives available.

In mother/son relationships, the woman plays the "older" one even if she is not chronologically older. In our experience the marriage of a younger man to a considerably older woman usually exemplifies mother/son-ing. On the other hand, we have had a number of cases where a woman much younger than her husband still assumes the role of mother. In any case, the mother adopts a "child" to whom she is both mother and father, and it is not uncommon for him to call her Mom or Momsy, as did the architect at the cocktail party. She is very often unaware of her own "feeling reaction" to life, and has buried her personal, human needs in her role. Her therapeutic task is to learn to experience and express her weakness which she has hidden behind her motherly strength, the principle of Eros within.

The son gets locked into a sexual relationship with a mother-provider, which keeps him infantile and dependent in areas where he must express his strength if he is to be fulfilled. Essentially, he needs to leave the womb, to release the breast, to cut the cord.

Ken came gradually to recognize his helpless kind of dependency. In reality he did not know Yvonne or she him. Each was surprised at the transformation of the other. Very probably they might have made it as husband and wife if they had been willing to go through a period of courtship and discovery. They elected not to. When Yvonne became involved in some psychological techniques similar to those employed with Ken, she, too, discovered feelings that had long been ignored. She had been afraid to be a woman. She had always been plump as a girl, not particularly sexy, and her father had often made fun of the fact that she didn't have dates. She got his attention by waiting on him around the house, cooking his favorite desserts, playing part-time mother. He had ridiculed her for going to college, and even made fun of Ken when she married him.

She had found much of her emotional freedom in her relationship with Dave. She was able to be confused, uncertain, to consult someone else, to rely on another's strength without losing her own. When the therapist had "strong" Yvonne engage in a dialogue with "weak" Yvonne, she touched upon deep and forgotten feelings that flooded out with anger and tears. When she began to shout: "Sometimes I need someone, too. SOMETIMES I HURT AND I'M AFRAID," she was asked whom she was shouting at. "My dad," she said, "My dad . . . and Ken." "Why don't you tell them that you are going to be you?" the therapist said. "It's time you told them who you really are." She paused for a moment. Her face was flushed, her whole body seem to shake.

"I'm a woman, damn it. I'M A WOMAN — A REAL WOMAN! — and I want a MAN, a MAN, not a grinning, apologetic, gentle little baby boy. I want a MAN. And finally I've GOT ONE, AND HE LOVES ME LIKE I AM. I'm not going to be anyone's goddamn mother except the kids, and they can take care of themselves now. I WANT A MAN." "You won't let him be a man," said the therapist. "IF HE'S A MAN, I WON'T HAVE A THING TO SAY ABOUT IT. DAVE DOESN'T ASK MY PERMISSION. He just is one, and I love him."

Yvonne was helped a great deal by a body awareness program that was offered to her in the therapeutic setting. She recognized how she had hidden her breasts in her arms and shoulders, how her extra weight was somehow related to her role as supermother. She learned to love her own body, and it showed. Many of her controls were also visible around her mouth and in her neck. She learned to let go and her whole expression went through a kind of transformation. Her jaw muscles became relaxed; the lines around her mouth softened and disappeared.

Perhaps Ken and Yvonne could have made it successfully as husband and wife. Perhaps the patterns of behavior established between them were so rigid that it would have been too painful and difficult to change. It doesn't matter, because they did what they wanted to do, and the dissolution of a mother/son relationship freed two people to know a new kind of joy.

It was not Ken's *fault* really that Yvonne was a mother to him, nor was it Yvonne's *fault* that Ken was a perennial son. The whole involvement was not a matter of *fault* but of *fact*. Yvonne was, indeed, a super-mother, and Ken was a super-son. Neither wanted to remain in the role. Each resented it. Their marriage had simply confirmed a role that had already been assumed. They had not blindly entered into a relationship. They had begun the relationship because it felt good, and as they lived together, they accepted it, like most men and women, not really believing that they had any right to do something about it. The marriage only reinforced the mother/son relationship with which they had begun their marriage.

Nor would it make sense to *blame* their parents. They discovered that their parents did the best they knew how. Forgiving their parents was an important step in their maturation. It was really a way of assuming responsibility for their own behavior and not blaming it on someone else. This was perhaps the most important thing they were taught in therapy. The decision to *be* different was their own, as indeed, was the pain and work necessary to bring this about. The therapeutic framework merely created an environment in which it was safe to be the persons that they really were.

We live in an environment which reinforces the mother/son relationship, even as it reinforces other unhealthy unions. The puritan environment even encourages such couples to remain in their union and attempts to punish them if they dissolve it. The "Till death do us part" syndrone is frequently extolled as a mark of maturity, courage, and inner strength. Perhaps, even more often, it is a mark of fear, of social pressure, of a dearth of personal freedom. Modern man is rapidly recognizing that it is his first and foremost right to be free and responsible for his own behavior. His life belongs to him even as does his behavior. He does not have to remain in a union which is painful and destructive. He owes it to himself as a person to become what he already is — to let his own real personhood emerge.

The mother/son relationship of Ken and Yvonne was not a love relationship. It was *phony,* artificial, because neither was being real. It was a manipulative relationship. Ken got affection and attention by being a boy. He wanted love, he had always wanted it, and his boyishness was his fierce and controlling way of demanding it. His helplessness was, in its way, contrived. It was the easy way out. It made unnecessary the pain of maturation. It was a kind of unwritten contract: "I will be a boy so that you will love me without making demands on me." But he wasn't loved, and he knew it. He had never taken the risk of love. He was afraid of it. But there was nothing really gentle about his boyishness. It was a boyishness of steel. It forbade Yvonne the freedom to get angry, to depend on someone, to open up and speak from her heart. It denied her the right to be weak, to lose control, to panic. It is true, she could have done these things, but there was a little boy who consistently refused her the right. To take it in spite of him would have required immense courage. And when she met Dave, her womanhood exploded in his arms and the stored-up feelings of the years seemed to dissolve her.

And Yvonne's motherhood, too, was a manipulation. It said consistently, "Look and see how accomplished I am, what I do for you, how stupid and ungainly you are." To remain a boy was Ken's way of avoiding a conflict, of feeling the pain of Yvonne's perpetual putdown. He had learned to laugh instead of crying, to grin instead of screaming, to shuffle and bow his head instead of choking her as she was choking him. They were locked in a painful relationship that appeared comfortable. Only under the surface did they know the pain.

Ken knew the pain of the children who did not take him seriously, of the other men that won his wife's admiration, the doctor, the clergyman, the professor in extension courses. Yvonne knew the pain of her

own frumpiness, of his passive hands that ritualisti-
cally sought her sexuality, hands that could easily be
put off as she tested him and accepted his cunning
boyishness, and Yvonne knew the pain of her rejection.

These were not nice, gentle, successful people as the
neighbors thought, as the social group insisted. It was
not another "perfect" marriage. These were conniving,
bleeding, frightened, pained, lonely, manipulating,
hurting human beings who had already given in to the
layer of death. Life was over, never to return. They
were not a son and his eternal mother, but a lonely
man and hungry woman who had lost contact with
their pain even as they had lost contact with their
yearning for love.

To watch them begin to realize that they did not
have to remain in the roles that life had provided, to
watch them discover that the love they longed for
could be had in reality, to see them pour out the pain
that had been stored up since childhood, to see their
very faces and bodies change to express more freely
the new force of life — all of this was to know that
man can make more of life than a sterile compromise
with the fear and meaninglessness that surrounds him.
A mother and son in marriage can become a man and
woman — if they believe it is truly their right and are
willing to experience the pain of personal growth. Thus
we believe that a mother/son relationship can become
a *mutually nourishing* one wherein each can be a giver

and receiver, each strong and weak. To grow from the rigid patterns described herein is not an easy task, but it is possible through awareness. *Awareness creates change,* and the awareness of mothers and sons can change a rigid relationship into *an alive and exciting encounter.*

Chapter 5

The Supporting Relationship: Daddies and Dolls

In many ways, the daddy/doll relationship is not a relationship at all. It is two people living together playing very complex roles. The writings of Henrik Ibsen, especially in *A Doll's House,* suggest the presence of this pattern in our culture. As shown in Figure 1 the daddy/doll relationship is the reverse of the mother/son relationship because in this case the man plays the role of strength and the woman that of weakness. Each is a kind of cultural distortion of masculinity and femininity. The man appears to be strong. He is suave, intelligent, cool, charming, personable, usually succesful, apparently confident and in control of every situation. In the stereotype, he sits calmly with his pipe in his mouth surveying the world and his little doll is more than willing to sit on his lap and accept his help and direction. Actually, he is not as strong as he is uninvolved in the relationship. His doll is his mannequin who frames his masculinity well, who, in a sense, establishes and supports it. She is not a person to him as much as she is an expensive plaything. He does not reveal to her his weakness, since his image depends on his revelation of strength. In reality, the doll is usually a much stronger person. She controls the relationship by exaggerating her weakness and dependency. She can whine and pout and smile her way into power. She is usually sexy to behold in a kind of hybrid cross between Lolita and Marilyn Monroe. Very often, however, she is not really involved sexually. She would be inclined to feign an orgasm because her image would demand that she have one. But she is not at all "letting go" in the relationship. She is holding the reins tight with childish manipulation. The daddy and his doll actually avoid each other; they pass in the hall, they do not make contact as persons.

The daddy/doll relationship often occurs in the June and December association. It occurs often in a man's second marriage, after he has "made it" and looks for someone to approve, or even adore, his new-found success of the middle years. He has arrived, and he needs the doll image to complete the picture of his achievement. And the doll needs him. He pays her the fatherly attention that she likely never received. He buys her the clothes, the jewelry, takes her to the places that give her a sense of well being. He permits her to remain uninvolved and in control. She never has to know the kind of masculine maturity that may well inaugurate the passage of the female from childhood to womanhood. She remains "unconquered," detached, often superficial, protected, environmentally secure. She does not have to know the painful process of creating inner strength.

Very often the daddy/doll marriage is "successful." It works. The psychologist can view it as a failure of two individuals to relate honestly and really, and he is probably objectively correct. But they often get along, especially in a second marriage. They enjoy traveling and frequent, extravagant entertaining. They are happy together because, as in many immature relationships, the right kind of neurotic balance is achieved and sustained. Daddy and his doll can enjoy the comfort of his or her respective sexuality because it is sustained by a well defended stereotype and resists any challenge. In reality there often is a quality of sexual passivity in the relationship.

Joe, a successful internist of thirty-seven, married Sandy, who was twenty-eight. It was a first marriage for both. Joe had an elaborate bachelor's pad in an exclusive condominium and a variety of masculine hobbies. He was an accomplished hunter, not only of ducks and pheasants and quail, but also of big game, and had made a trip to South America to pursue the jaguar. He had bagged his tiger in Asia. He skied, flew his own plane, dressed exquisitely, was an active sports fan, played a good game of golf, and gambled heavily. He had dated hundreds of attractive girls, none of them for too long a time. His sexual drive, surprisingly to most of the girls, was moderate. To the variety of dolls that he dated, his sexual "control" was a relief. Most of them were accustomed to fighting off men. Joe never embarrassed them. Often he wanted sex very early in the relationship, usually the first night, but once he had made his conquest he was seldom pushy again. He was a great conversationalist, had a variety of interests, treated his dates with great polish and respect. He was Hugh Heffner's dream man with a direct line to the Playgirl of the Month. His name appeared often in a spicy social column in the paper, and he was considered, year after year, the catch of the season.

Sandy had landed him by playing it cool. She caught him at the right time. The dating game was growing tiresome for him. And Sandy was elusive. She had refused to sleep with him for almost six weeks after they began to date. Finally, he had practically raped her in his apartment. Since Joe did not commit himself in any way to her, she made a point to date others. This irritated Joe no end. He was not accustomed to this. She also paid a great deal of attention to other men, and Joe was upset on more than one occasion. Ultimately she would be his doll, but unlike the other faceless beauties he had dated, she had to be won. Within six months after the first date, they were married. And she was ready to be his doll.

They traveled through Europe, journeyed by ship to tropical Mexico and Hawaii, went to Tahiti, the Bahamas, flew regularly to Vegas, and appeared often in pictures on the society page. Sandy was unquestionably the best dressed woman in the area. His gifts of jewelry were elaborate and much talked about. Their marriage was the envy of every couple who knew them. Therapy began for them when Sandy sought help for a problem of "frigidity." Joe was upset at her lack of sexual interest. Their sex life had become routine and empty. The problem began about two years after they were married. Joe had invested a large sum in a real estate development program. It had floundered badly, and he lost almost half of his investment. A much publicized malpractice suit had also caused him personal pain and public embarrassment. The cool image was threatened, and he began making demands on Sandy that she had never known from him before. He wanted sex more often, he required comforting, he wanted to talk about his problems, his personal fears, his desire to get away. He was drinking heavily.

She refused him any sexual contact when he was drunk, complied reluctantly and passively to his more frequent sexual demands when he was sober and hurting. Daddy seemed to be disintegrating. He complained about her expenditures of money, revoked several of her charge accounts, and openly began having affairs with several young nurses. She retaliated by coming on strong sexually to other men. Joe was wild with jealousy. Their fights were loud and frequent. Even after a violent argument, Joe seldom seemed satisfied. When he finally came into a therapy program himself, he admitted that Sandy won most of the arguments. He began to recognize the strength born of her detachment from the relationship and complained bitterly: "She really doesn't give a damn." On several occasions he had slapped her, and she had gone into an hysterical tantrum each time. On a couple of occasions she had assumed a kind of fetal crouch and screamed for several minutes. Finally they separated. At first, Joe could not bear the separation for more than a few days. The brief reunion would be loving and comforting. The complexion of the relationship seemed to change, and it had the dominant qualities of a mother/son association. But Sandy could not sustain this role for long. She needed her daddy, and when he wasn't there, she became a pouting bitch. She was uncomfortable with Joe's weakness and called it feminine, which threw him, in his vulnerable condition, into an uncontrollable rage and out the door. Finally after a series of breakups and reunions, the separation became more permanent, and each began seriously to work in therapy.

Fortuitiously, beneath the role playing, there were two people who did seem to have some basic attraction for each other. Joe began to realize that he had largely identified with his mother at home. His father was kind of a vague specter who made a great deal of money; his mother was a warm, comforting, almost doting protectress. Joe shared with her a kind of special intimacy and was devoted to her delicate "femininity." He also began to recognize that his mother had prevented him from having a relationship with his father. He was able to question the authenticity of his feelings for his mother and to discover that in great part they were artificial. In a series of psychological exercises, he was able to express his anger towards his mother and the sadness he felt for his father. He began, little by little, to see them as people. And as they came into focus as persons, Joe began to have a clearer picture of himself, and then of Sandy.

Sandy recognized that she had manipulated her father for his attention and affection, that in reality she did not at all feel accepted by him. In her mature years, he had been disappointed that she had not married. She discovered a seductive kind of pattern in her relationship to all men, and accepted the fact of her great strength as a person under the guise of the helpless girl. She also began to understand her refusal to let Joe's weakness show. And her sweet, girlish ways made it difficult for Joe to express his anger directly and consistently. He had resorted to occasional explosive outbursts when he could not longer contain himself. Frequently, his anger came out as pouting and stubborn silence — which only increased Sandy's contempt.

Joe and Sandy were two bright, sensitive people, who made great progress. They did a series of exercises together learning to fight directly, learning to recognize the polarity of their own strength and weakness. Sandy had hidden her strength, and Joe had denied his weakness. (See Figure 2.) The elaborate role playing had only fortified the dishonesty of each of them. Gradually, they were able to see one another as persons and to relate rhythmically. Ultimately, they moved out of the area, later adopted a child, and at last contact seemed to be doing reasonably well.

It is not uncommon to see the daddy/doll relationship in the first marriage of young people. A young man, we'll name him Bob, complained that his wife Kathy could not tolerate being alone at night. She was desperately afraid of the dark and felt that she was being watched or would be attacked. Often during the day she suffered long periods of despondency and cried for hours on end. She could not seem to get enough sleep. The evenings, however, were the most problematic. Bob was working two jobs and often left Kathy alone at night. Several times he had been obliged to leave work to return home to comfort her.

Bob was patient, attentive, understanding. Rarely did he get angry.

When Kathy came in, the therapist found it hard to believe that she was twenty-three years old. She appeared to be about eighteen, talked with an exceptionally whiney voice, and went from giggling to tears in rapid outbursts. Her giggling was diluted with anxiety, and her tears were fringed with an underlying anger. Actually, she seldom admitted or permitted any kind of anger. She was a prototype of the young doll. She had quit her job at the beginning of the marriage, and her daddy, Bob, had encouraged her in the decision, although she had little to do around the house. She spent a great deal of time being the super-wife. She planned the meals with great pains, eagerly demanded his reaction to and greeted every failure with tears. She needed Bob's assistance with everything she did, constantly sought his advice, admired his opinions and mouthed them as her own.

In their courtship there had been few tears. She had met Bob at college, admired his idealism and progressive views of social reform. She was impressed by his devotion to economic success and by his well-rounded confidence. She loved to be held and caressed for hours on end, was most compliant with his wishes, and created circumstances which kept him almost constantly by her side. He helped her with term papers and tracked down references for her in the library.

On one occasion, he even talked to one of her professors about a questionable grade. He reminded her to have the oil changed in her car, bought her presents he could not afford, took her out for dinner in places which strained his budget unbearably.

Kathy, who had worked for a year before they got married, spent her money almost entirely on clothes. Frequently she bought things for Bob, and at Christmas she embarrassed him with the number of gifts she gave him. He felt compelled to do as well in return but could not outdo her in any way. Sexually, before marriage she did everything to please him. Shortly after marriage, she told him that she felt used sexually, that he didn't really care for her, that he only wanted her body. She said it sadly, with many tears. Bob backed off and spent more time caressing her and rubbing his little girl's back. Kathy admitted that she often spent a great deal of time in bed during the afternoons when Bob was gone. She enjoyed romantic tales of every sort, masturbated with regularity and frequency, sometimes engaging in elaborate ritual. She had known abundant sexual relationships with girlfriends with whom she had stayed overnight when she was in her junior high school years. She sometimes dreamed about homosexual relationships with older women. On increasingly frequent occasions, her sex with Bob was a kind of mutual masturbation, similar to the love making of their courtship days. Kathy had been raised as a Catholic and had great difficulty permitting intercourse before marriage. The masturbation did not seem to make her guilty — only depressed.

Bob was ambitious and exceedingly controlled. His voice was a resonant monotone. He spoke quietly, kindly, patiently. He had, of course, called the therapist to make the first appointment for Kathy, and after her first visit, he approached like a concerned father inquiring about the problem with his delicate daughter. There was only time to explore briefly Kathy's relationship with her father, since she ceased coming after about five or six visits. Bob only agreed to come twice. He was certain that it was entirely Kathy's problem and that it was his job to protect her. Actually, she stopped therapy at his insistence. She had reported to him that her therapist was mean to her, that he had been angry and impatient. Bob decided to look elsewhere for more considerate help.

She had managed to get in touch with some of her anger and to recognize the manipulative whininess of her voice. She was able to see some of her fear of the dark and her sense of loneliness as a manipulation of Bob to spend more time with her. Bob was able to cut down on the hours he spent at work and more or less adjust his life to the needs of his doll. This, of course, reinforced his role as daddy. On his second and last visit, he indicated that Kathy was a very sensitive, delicate person, and that he was going to make a renewed effort to be patient with her tears. He also insisted that he did not detect any whininess in her voice and expressed thanks for all the help that had been given. "It's one of those personality clashes," he said, on leaving, "she's the same way with a couple of my friends."

Bob and Kathy will likely make it, at least for several years, in a sustaining daddy/doll relationship. Friends will speak regularly of their great devotion for each other. And Kathy will whine her way to continued victories while Bob feels his own growing strength. Man's capacity to adjust is incredible.

At times, the daddy/doll relationship can seem liberating and productive of great, individual creativity on the part of the spouses. Don and Cynthia are both in a second marriage. He is, perhaps, fifty and she about thirty-eight. Each has a profession, Don as a builder and property developer, Cynthia as an interior decorator. Each of them owns his own business. On the job, Cynthia is cold, calculating, hard as nails, and very successful. In her relationship with Don, she is a purring, sexy doll. When he looks at her, he beams. He is the proud father who delights in showing her off to the world. In his presence Cynthia has difficulty making decisions, can hardly use a can-opener with efficiency. Continually she asks: "Don, will you help me with this?" In her profession, she asks help from no one. Don delights in talking about her beauty, takes great pride in her vast wardrobe, treats her with deference and delicacy. She is his precious flower, and he is her defender from the world. When he teases her in conversation socially, she becomes flustered and embarrassed. When she is teased on other occasions, she is quick witted and cynical. She slides in and out of her roles with incredible ease. She is almost like two different people. Her business drive is fed by some secret energy which never appears in her role as Don's doll. And there is no reason to expect that the marriage will not work out marvelously for each of them. Each is clever, capable, a superbly functioning person, and has few, if any, doubts about the quality of the daddy/doll relationship. Nor will anyone ever have a chance to unsettle them.

On social occasions, when some devotee of instant and evangelical therapy had returned from a weekend encounter with a missionary fervor to free the world, he "encountered" Don and Cynthia at a cocktail party with a series of newly discovered techniques. It was beautiful to watch Don grin and say: "I'll get around to that in my next marriage." Cynthia snuggled up to him like a kitten and purred: "I'll never let you out of my sight, and I'll kill the one who tries to take you away."

From our research, it is apparent that unless the relationship grows, the daddy and doll fall into the following traps:

The daddy takes on the role of father-protector-provider in the face of his doll's feminine helplessness. He provides security and she is his exceptional and delightfully entertaining child.

The doll never matures. She has found an ability to control the man in her poor-little-helpless-me posture. She is the undercat who always wins. She cries, plays naive, stupid and helpless and makes the man feel responsible for her.

Daddies often seem to identify with their mothers, sometimes taking on the mother role with their wives. Daddies are very often maternal husbands. They are frequently controlled and moralistic when who have little genuine spontaneity. This was true in the case of Joe, the internist, for example, despite his vast interests and accomplishments. The doll wife is often a "foreign minister" socially. She also functions as a "sex queen," but is generally not very interested in sex.

Daddies often develop no great sexual drive, and this endears them to the dolls who want to be regarded for their personality and achievement rather than for their beauty and appearance alone. Dolls often feel victimized or used sexually when not relating with an authentic daddy.

Dolls often become feaful if left alone at night, fearing darkness, prowlers, bats, etc. A doll identifies with her daddy's successes, and her life is centered very regularly around clothes, home possessions, vacations, elaborate parties.

The doll finds in her daddy the security that she never received as a child. She gives affection and deference in much the same manner she did as a child.

The doll has never released herself from her father. Her task in maturation is to recognize and express her strength, and to stop hiding behind her weakness. (See Figure 2.)

Yet, our recent research and experience has shown that the daddy/doll relationship is in no way hopeless. It can become the relationship of a mature man and woman, if they become aware of one another and find the rhythm of their strength and weakness. We have seen many cases where each has learned to find his own substance or footing as a person and in so doing has recognized the new potential and beauty in the other as well. But each person must become responsible for his or her own personal growth and then relate as person to person rather than daddy to doll. As individual growth takes place, the relationship also grows and becomes mutually supportive and exciting.

We do not believe that the sexes will disappear in a kind of androgynous compromise to reduce the creative tension of life. But, hopefully, with increasing humanism, there can be cultivated an atmosphere in which the daddy/doll relationship can grow beyond a manipulative dependency into the creative and honest love of an adult man and woman.

Chapter 6

The Challenging Relationship: Bitches and Nice Guys

The bitch/nice guy relationship is the real prototype of the unhappy American marriage. The writings of James Thurber have cleverly lampooned this pattern. It is the butt of a thousand jokes, the best material of the stand-up, story-telling comedian. It is good humor because so many in the audience can identify with it. In reality, the bitch/nice guy relationship is one in which the rhythmic expression of love and anger has rigidified. The bitch has exaggerated her expression of anger, the nice guy has exaggerated his expression of love. Freud indeed spoke of the duality of love and hate in the human relationship, and the Greeks noted that Eros is the child of Ares and Aphrodite — indicating that Eros is born of anger and love. But when the balance between the expression of love and anger is lost, when the enticement and creative beauty in a relationship is gone, it is not unusual to behold the genesis of a bitch/nice guy relationship.

Harold and Jane had been married for fourteen years. They had one child, a daughter of twelve. They are intelligent, rather well off in an upper middle-class bracket, and live in a beautiful home which Harold designed. He is a succesful architect — quiet, shy, and seemingly gentle. Jane is a social worker with a flair for the artistic. She paints rather well, knows colors and fabrics, and is concerned about the poor and the dispossessed. She is expressive, outspoken, and tells long, elaborate stories about her social experiences with the welfare cases she has visited in the past. She has not worked at her profession for almost ten years.

They came into therapy when Jane discovered that Harold was having an affair. In private discussion, he admitted that he had taken a number of women to bed without much significance until he met a bright, young designer who seemed to appreciate him. He had abruptly broken off the relationship at Jane's insistence but was miserable without Dawn. He did not want a divorce because he thought it would have an ill effect on his daughter, Debbie. He began again to sleep around a bit without great satisfaction and was angry at himself. He felt that he could make the marriage work. It would be very disappointing to his parents to admit that he had failed; it would, he felt, affect his business to bear the public shame of a divorce in a somewhat narrow community, and he had just expanded his offices and taken on additional staff. He was miserable, but he was a nice guy.

His sex life with Jane had been doled out over the past several years when he behaved properly. At such times he was very aggressive sexually and felt like a man. But usually, the next morning or the same night, he would take the risk of talking to Jane, and she would put him down. She had often told him that he was weak, that people in the office made a fool of him and took advantage of him, that he spent too much time away from home, that he had neglected Debbie, or on other occasions, that he was spoiling her. She interrupted him when he spoke, criticized what he wore, and responded to his occasional outbursts of enthusiasm with sullenness. She often threatened to leave, to live in another area where the people weren't so "snooty," where Debbie could eventually meet someone worthwhile. She complained that she had given up her career to make him a home and that he was never there to enjoy it. And when he was home, he had nothing to say. She rebuked him for not fighting, and when he made some effort to do so, she lashed back with continual fury until he again fell into silence.

Occasionally he would explode violently, but only at rare intervals. One time, when they were driving to a party and he had come home a few minutes late from work, she began harassing him about "getting a move on." She directed the turns he made, complained about the way he slouched at the wheel, reminded him that he shouldn't drink too much if he were going to drive home. He was silent until he came to the host's home. He stopped and said: "I'm not going in. What time do you want me to pick you up?" She was furious. Surprisingly, he yelled at her: "Get out! You can get a ride home!" She got out docilely and stared at him as he drove away. When she reached home, he was already in bed and feigned sleep. He noted that she was cautious and quiet getting in bed. The next morning she began to pout and didn't say anything for almost three days. He responded by being a nice guy.

When Harold came into counseling he appeared controlled and nervous. He spoke softly, smiled shyly and seemed most appreciative for the attention given him. In continuing sessions, he spoke more freely, and the genuine charm of his personality gave his face greater strength. He spoke of a childhood in which his father, an insensitive, boorish man, kept the family in continual fear and tension. He spoke warmly of his mother, who took the time to listen to him. He had not dated much in high school, was a good student, and had gotten on well with everyone. He was ambitious, determined to succeed, and saved his money to establish his own firm. His unique creativity surprised everyone. He was almost thirty before he married Jane. She was barely twenty and treated him as if he were a king. She completed her schooling during the first years of marriage and was pregnant with Debbie when she received her degree.

She had been shy and seemingly warm, and was most attentive to his wishes. She seemed happy to be with him. At first she had been uncomfortable with his friends, many of whom were sophisticated and arty. But gradually she felt somewhat more comfortable. Harold didn't exactly know when the change in her personality took place. He thought, perhaps, it began when Debbie was about a year old. It was almost at the same time that he was going in on his own. The new business required extra time and attention. At first, Jane seemed to understand. Then he noticed that she was complaining a great deal about the demands that Debbie made on her. "It's great for you," she said, "You just play with her an hour or so a day. I have her all the time." A short time later, Jane wanted to take a job outside the home. She was tired of being a housewife and baby sitter. She worked in a welfare office and an elderly woman, Mrs. Davis, lived in with the family. Harold felt guilty about time he spent away from home, and felt that there was a barrier between himself and Jane that he had never noticed before. He could not make any demands on her now that she was working and Mrs. Davis was looking after the shopping and the meals. He took Jane out for dinner two or three times a week, but their time together was unpleasant. No matter what restaurant he decided upon, she would have a different idea. If he asked her where she would like to go, she said coldly, "It's up to you." If he picked a place, she was dissatisfied.

Most of her conversation was a complaint about her job. So many people wanted something for nothing. Or the whole welfare system was ineffectual. Or no one really cared about the poor. She was critical of service in the restaurants, and she asked for food to be recooked — things which she had never done before. During this same period, of course, their sex life deterioriated. Harold had never really looked at another woman, although he was surrounded by a number of attractive women in his work. He had first become involved with a woman at a convention in San Francisco. The experience was overwhelming. She had actually liked him, liked to hear him talk. He thought he was in love, but since the woman lived some 2,000 miles away, there was no real possibility of getting together. He called her a few times and then gradually let it drop. Once he planned to spend a weekend with her, but Jane had demanded that they get away together. It had been miserable.

Occasionally there were good times, but Harold could not really let himself go. He was afraid of her temper. It was sudden and explosive, and he couldn't really fight back. If he argued, she argued louder and longer. If he persisted, she locked herself in her room and wouldn't talk for days. When she decided to talk again, he was ready and submissive. The bitch had won again and wallowed in her anger and misery.

At work Harold had met Dawn, who had been one of his creative assistants for several years. She was barely out of college when she came to the firm, and he had known her for almost four years before they got involved. Dawn adored him, found him affectionate and whimsical, humorous and sensitive, attentive and profoundly intelligent. She knew something of his field and appreciated his quiet kind of genius. They had an affair which lasted for almost four years until Jane discovered it and demanded that Harold fire Dawn or she would file for divorce. He fired Dawn and broke off the relationship. By this time he had withdrawn almost entirely from the marriage relationship. His involvement with Jane was minimal. She was not able to hurt him to the extent that she had a few years ago. He was still afraid of her but could ward off her angry words and hostile innuendos. She sensed his emotional withdrawal and became more direct and blatant in her angry denunciations. He had a series of intermittent and discreet liaisons with women. But his once boyish face, with the bright, sad, perceptive eyes, began to look jowlish and dissipated. His shoulders, never broad, were now narrow and pinched and his frame was bent forward.

Harold was not really a nice guy, as it began to appear in counseling sessions. His niceness was his way of fighting by refusing to get involved. Actually, he won most of the fights, and he knew it. He was afraid to fight directly. He could not tolerate violent anger and loud, prolonged battles. He fought a cold war and the flak that Jane threw at him almost continually only increased his coldness and expanded the depths of his rage. In therapy, the rage began to come out. It was sheer fury, murderous, hate-filled, long-buried anger. First he challenged his father in a bitter diatribe. He stamped on his grave and demanded that he come back so that he could beat him back into the ground. The he started in on Jane and called her every angry name that his vocabulary and psyche permitted. He slapped her in effigy and demanded that she sit down and shut up, even though she was not present. Finally he began to release his anger and contempt for himself. His weak, mealy-mouthed, silent, passive self engaged in a battle with his angry, hostile, contemptuous self. The war was waged fiercely. At one point it appeared he might destroy some of the furniture, which had been made hardy enough in anticipation of such events. Then, his anger spent, he began to cry the torrents of tears that he had held back since childhood. He sobbed convulsively, some times fighting angrily in the midst of flowing tears, pleading with his father, with Jane, with himself. Then the tears came quietly, and he desperately asked for love. In reality, Jane never could have matched his anger. His silence would have lasted longer than her invectives and complaints. The anger was as fierce and strong as the flood of tears that it held back. He had built a fortress for his own survival.

Later on in therapy he began to recognize that his relationship with Dawn bore great resemblance to his early relationship with Jane. Dawn was in awe of him as Jane had been, she was delighted by his expensive gifts, she liked the prestige of going to important and expensive places where she had never been before. He was introducing her to life. She was most compliant sexually, as Jane had been. It was the beginning of another daddy/doll relationship, the kind of relationship that frequently is transformed into a bitch/nice guy confrontation. When the daddy decides to have a wife and the doll must grow up to relate to a husband, then the new dynamic comes into force. When Jane began pouting like a doll and did not get the predicated response from Harold, she became the spoiled bitch. Very likely, had he married Dawn, without therapeutic help, he would have developed the same kind of relationship. We have known clients who have repeated the same dynamic four times over without success.

Sessions with Jane revealed that she had not always been a bitch. She was from a rather poor background, and she was devoted to her father, who seemed to play her against his wife. She was the only girl with two brothers in the family. She wanted to marry well to please her father, and when Harold arrived in his Chrysler, her father was duly impressed. Jane was always proud of Harold during their courtship. He knew what to do. He could talk to headwaiters, order different kinds of wine, and speak a little French when it was required. Her friends were dazzled by his soft charm and gentle manliness. He had the real savoir faire. He treated Jane with great delicacy. He was thoughtful, often brought gifts, and never complained about money. When later in marriage he accused her of being a spendthrift, she was flabbergasted.

Jane had dreamed of meeting a man like Harold. She had dated a number of young men, and was sexually very appealing with her effulgent body and her little girl ways. She had intercourse with a number of men but never really got very involved. She was concerned about being different from other girls. She wanted to be respected for her intelligence and conversational ability. She wanted attention. Usually she got it and was the center of focus at a great number of parties. She never lacked an escort, and although she rarely had an orgasm (possibly once before marriage), she liked sex. She loved to show Harold off to her friends. It was when they began to travel in his circle of acquaintances that she first noticed her discomfort.

He did not seem to pay as much attention to her. There were experiences that he had shared with others that she had not been a part of. "Remember the time ..." at parties became a signal to her that she was going to be left out. Many of the parties centered around the architectural field. She knew very little about this, and although she was artistic and creative in her way, she was not in the same league with Harold's friends. They knew something of the theater, discussed the meaning of various kinds of music, talked about Spanish and Oriental art in great depth. She was unnerved. Occasionally she would talk about her work in welfare but no one really seemed interested. She felt Harold's embarrassment at her inadequacy. He didn't seem to want her to talk. He wanted her merely to be there to frame his presence in her sensuous beauty.

Occasionally she had feelings for other men, but she denied them and was angry at Harold for squelching her career. Actually she was afraid of the other men she met at parties. They were calm and confident, bright and aggressive, and she would not have been able to fend them off. She was uncomfortable in conversation with them. She said that she just wanted Harold to be proud of her, and she wanted to feel his protection in these difficult circumstances. Actually she never admitted her discomfort. She had been playing a game with him ever since their courtship began. She did not feel that she was his equal, and she felt that he would reject her if he discovered this. She did everything she could to keep up.

She continued her education and then later blamed him for forcing her to go to work, even though he had not in any way suggested that she complete her schooling. Harold was always to blame. She projected more and more of her feelings onto him. Her own weakness became his weakness, her own dullness at parties became his, her own feeling that she was not socially acceptable made him a careless dresser. Actually Harold handled himself well in these social situations and was quite comfortable. He also dressed well, but under the onslaught of Jane's complaints, he began to wonder about himself. Rapidly, the sexy doll of a warm courtship was becoming an intricate and unmitigated bitch.

Jane had few friends. She had not been able to sustain them, and she was not comfortable with the wives of Harold's friends. Her fear of people was expressed in her continual carping. She outlined in great detail the shortcomings of this one and that, which again was a desperate projection of her own feeling in company. Her whole approach to men had been a sexual, doll-like affection, and when this was no longer effective, she became critical of everyone she feared. In reality she was screaming for Harold's attention, and the more he turned her off, the more she screamed. She was in great pain. She knew his seething anger. She sensed it through his gentle coldness and quiet retreat from her. But it was not the kind of anger she could deal with. Harold no longer fought fair; he fought to win and to drive her from his back.

Actually Harold had never taken her seriously as a person. She was his doll, the sexy woman who made him feel like a man. When she asked more of him, he was not prepared to give it. He did not see her as a woman; he did not really feel married to her. She had been comfortable, supportive, loving and attentive, and now she was a bitch. She sensed his fear of divorce, she knew that she had him trapped. There was nothing he could do. So she continued to be a bitch, actually pushing him away, so desperately was she angry with herself. She did not really want him to go, but as often happens in marriages of this kind, she would not recognize it until after he was gone. Then suddenly, she would become an old woman, neurotic, afraid, withdrawn and bitter. She was still a beautiful woman but her face was drawn. Her mouth was pinched and had lost its full sensuality; her eyes were hurt and hard, and her brow was knotted in tension and control.

Once, in an important therapy session, her face softened, and she said: "I am such a bitch."

"I know you are," her therapist replied.

"I wish he would beat the hell out of me."

"You've certainly been demanding that. Do you want me to beat you?"

"You're stronger than he is," she replied.

"No, I'm not," he said honestly. "And I don't live with you. But you're really not a bitch at all. You just refuse to let your love and caring show. You're a frightened young woman."

"Yes, I'm frightened," she said sadly.

"You hold back your warmth and hide your hurt in

anger. You're not honest. Nor are you really a bitch. You're in constant pain."

"Is that why I can't have an orgasm any more?"

"I'm not in the orgasm business. You can have an orgasm if you let go of your anger and learn to express love. If you can learn to feel your tenderness, your orgasms will take care of themselves.

"What am I afraid of?"

"Now you're playing little girl with me. I won't be your daddy. What are you afraid of?"

"I'm afraid of losing Harold. And yet I don't know if I want him."

"I'm not sure if you even *see* Harold. I don't think either of you has seen or heard the other one for years — if ever."

Gradually Jane began to own her fears and to discover that her anger was her admission that love and tenderness were unacceptable. She was able to admit that her relationship with her father was manipulative and artificial, and she resolved to do something about it. She was able to take the initiative in making friends and to express love in her voice, in her body, on her face. The tension in her face began to disappear and she looked much younger. She began to dress like a woman in her mid-thirties and to take responsibility for her own feelings. Later she was able to admit to Harold the extent of her hurt. The last time they came to therapy, they had the beginning of a relationship. It is not certain they will make it. That is not important, however, because they will make it as individuals and will not be held in a marriage by fear or social pressure. Each knows a great deal more about himself and what constitutes a human relationship. Each has lost innumerable psychosomatic symptoms — arthritic pains, headaches, back pains, and fatigue.

Our research shows that at first glance the rigid bitch/nice guy relationship looks much like a mother/son pair. But it soon becomes clear that as women, bitches are somewhat better balanced than mothers. They are active, aggressive, practical, and *are often attractive to their husbands.*

Nice guys are *more nurturant* to their wives than are sons and can be aroused to action more readily. They seem to give their wives security and comfort by placating their irritability and "bitchiness."

Bitches more often than not have used their fathers as ego-models and often become somewhat tomboyish. They are not as giving as mothers and are ambivalent about femininity.

Whereas mothers are often unglamorous and sexually drab, bitches can be "prick teasers" who like masculine attention. Although many men are fearful of their hostility and temper, such passion is often attractive and sexually exciting to them. The whole relationship can be a challenging one.

Whereas mothers like keeping sons under their domination, bitches are strongly demanding that their nice guys be "men."

Both mother/son and bitch/nice guy pairings, however, are a combination of dominant wives and submissive husbands. Thus, both bitches and mothers like to appear more accomplished than their men.

Nice guys, more than any other men, have strong needs to be liked and make great effort to gain acceptance from everyone. They are indirect about their hostility and often enjoy needling their bitchy wives.

Our research also shows that the typical American family is now most often a role-reversed family with a strong, efficient woman and an undeveloped, "feminine" man. It is a "matriarchal" marriage. The unconscious part of this pattern is the denial, on the part of the bitch, of the need to *love* and be loved. A woman's anger and hostility is her defense against the vulnerability she feels in love. Her growth requires that she face her unconscious need to get comfortable with intimacy. The husband in this pairing requires that he get in touch with his anger or assertiveness. He needs to recognize the need for safety and security provided by the role of nice guy and to become aware of his aggressive anger.

Bitches are often afraid to go too far for fear the nice guy will seek out a younger and more attractive woman. So they back down at critical moments. They need their men for help and support during crises.

Bitchiness is often a way to avoid the *real* conflicts in a marriage, thereby preventing communication at the deeper levels where the aliveness and strength of each person is experienced. Bitches are afraid of such a *person to person* relationship.

The bitch and nice guy can grow toward a relationship which is mutually challenging, wherein each is assertive as well as loving. Growing toward this goal requires that they develop as persons and not remain rigidly locked in a parasitical relationship. It requires that each dare to admit his hunger for love and dare to hope for the joy and beauty of life which can be theirs.

In the tens of thousands of bitch/nice guy relationships, there is enough hostility to ignite a thousand wars. But for them to transform this hostility into honest anger and gentle love, it is necessary that they surrender to their own humanness. A destructive and manipulative union of hatred and hurt can become a dramatic relationship of rhythmic anger and love if the bitch and nice guy accept the challenge of a vital and creative relationship.

Chapter 7

The Educating Relationship: Masters and Servants

The master/servant relationship is not strictly native to American soil where the struggle for feminine liberation has been increasingly persistent and successful. Its cultural history reflects the "natural superiority" of men. It offers men and women a distinct and well-defined role in marriage. Man is of true consequence, he is to be feared, attended, never questioned, he is the infallible intellect, the demanding teacher, the strong and unyielding animal. Woman is his "help-mate," his attendant, the concerned, anxious-to-please, dutiful, obedient wife. St. Paul spoke to her clearly, and his words were traditionally a part of the marriage ritual: "Wives, obey your husbands . . . be

167

subject to him in all things even as to the Lord." The master/servant relationship has been immortalized in Shaw's *Pygmalion*, wherein Professor Henry Higgins transforms a servant girl, a street urchin, into a lady. In the *My Fair Lady* version of the play she returns to his side at the end and docilely brings him his slippers.

The master/servant relationship is often successful. In a sense it provides a great deal of freedom. It has the advantage of dispelling uncertainty in a relationship. Each party knows exactly how to behave under all circumstances. The man is able to feel strong and "masculine," and the woman can be dependent and devoted. The master is often faithful, is usually protective, and seldom considers divorce. The servant has no need to attract other men, has plenty to do, and can know great security and satisfaction. Such a relationship is constantly under threat in the present culture, but its roots lie deep in history and unquestionably it will survive and actually thrive for a long time to come.

Ministers often marry servants, as does any man who sees himself called to a God-given kind of work. Doctors, too, accustomed as they are to the devoted and unquestioning service of nurses, are frequently masters. It is not uncommon for them to marry nurses and to expect the same kind of treatment at home that they receive from patients and staff. Nurses know that the doctor is better educated, better informed, and better equipped to deal with emergencies. They are most critical of the doctor who does not know his work with confidence and dispatch. They are often devoted to the man who works magic with his medical skills, in spite of the fact that such "god-like" men are themselves often quite insecure. Their profession gives them the status that they need, the income that makes them feel worthwhile. They find it difficult to express tenderness; or if they are at all able to experience it, they are loath to reveal it to others.

The best servants are usually from large families where they had abundant responsibility for the care of small children or duties around the house. If they had brothers, the men were usually not called upon to do any of the menial, "feminine" tasks around the house. Often servants are from religious homes, and they have been carefully taught to know their place. They have been instructed to hide their sexual charms, to wear loose sweaters and modest skirts, to be competent cooks and housekeepers, to be excellent mothers or governesses, not to interefere with the more important, inscrutable work of men. It is especially important that they only reflect the opinions of their husbands, that they be careful not to engage in man's talk. Often enough they have been met with: "What the hell do women know about such things?"

Very often the servant has not attended college, or at least has not graduated. She was taught carefully at home that education is not necessary for a woman.

When she does complete college, she usually attends a small, perhaps religious, college, preferably of the all-girls variety. Education would more than likely make her resent her role as servant, because it would open her to new talents and personal creativity that would provide her with personality and individuality. She would develop some need to do her own thing. Yet, if she has grown up dependent enough in the shadow of a strong father, her education may not make a truly successful invasion into her dependency. She may fear her opportunity and responsibility as a woman and take the line of least resistance into the passive role of servant.

This particular relationship of master/servant usually does not appear with any frequency in the therapeutic setting. When the servant type does appear, to complain of her husband's drinking or his unfaithfulness, she is usually afraid to tell her husband that she made an appointment without his permission. She will pay the bill out of money that she has set aside. When she does inform him that she is seeking advice, he usually refuses to cooperate unless she grows strong enough to threaten him with divorce. The servant type will usually be satisfied with "symptom-solving" and has no need to explore the relationship at any great depth. If the master becomes more controlled in his drinking or promises never to be unfaithful again — which usually means to be more careful — she feels that she has been successful. In her initial visit, she is often convinced that she has caused the problem by some personal omission.

Helen, a woman of fifty, came to complain about her husband's drinking problem. Al was a great financial success, a molder of men, and drove himself without consideration. He had struggled with a drinking problem most of his life. His whole approach to life was almost addictive. He worked feverishly, then he took time off completely — once for almost a year. He joined AA for a couple of years and did not drink at all. He was on and off the wagon for several years. When Helen came for help, he had been drinking helplessly for several months. She said she could not take it any longer. It was bearable when the children were home, but now they refused to live at home even though they were not yet married. There were four children in all, the youngest a senior in high school; and even he had decided to go away to school for his last year.

Al had tried everything to make the children live at home. He had refused an older son and daughter tuition money for college, but they had preferred to work and to take what their mother had been able to provide. The oldest daughter was living with an artist and working as a receptionst in a doctor's office. The oldest son, a senior in college, had conferred with the therapist at his mother's suggestion. He told of his fear of his father, of the numberless lectures he had heard, of the pressure put on him to conform to his father's opinions. He admitted to having nothing but contempt and hatred for his father. He pitied his mother, to whom he felt very close, but could not bring himself to live at home even though he felt she needed someone. He advised her to get a divorce.

Helen could not bring herself to desert Al at his time of need. She felt that if she had other interests, she would not be so bothered by his drinking. But she felt incapable of getting a job. She was not trained for anything; her whole life had centered in the family. She had been an outstanding homemaker and was always available to be the children's confidante. Each of them had a great devotion to her. She was the buffer, the emissary to the father when the children requested anything unusual. They were afraid to approach him. With the children all gone from home, she had approached Al about her going to work. He had laughed at her, "What the hell for? You've got everything you need!" When she persisted, he offered to provide work for her, to get a job for her in one of his friends' companies but she was dissatisfied with this.

After several sessions, she realized that she had no life of her own. When he no longer needed her except as a nurse on the morning after, when the children were able to be on their own, there was nothing left. She had not made many friends because Al had been critical of her choice of women. He did not want them "hanging around the house" when he came home. He wanted every breath of Helen's attention. His recreation and hobbies did not include her. He was an active kind of man when he was not overwhelmed with his alcoholic problem. He liked hunting and fishing and was a good golfer, but never included Helen in any of his days and weeks with the boys. He had taken his vacations with other men on hunting trips or golf excursions. She was glad to see him take some time off because he worked so hard. She was content to care for the children, to knit and sew, to try new recipes, to engage in volunteer work for the church and the art museum.

Gradually she began to experience her anger and to recognize that she wanted a life of her own, that she was a person who was something more than a portable clinic for her husband. When Al recognized her growing strength, he finally came to visit the therapist. He immediately took charge of the interview and shifted the focus onto his wife: "You're doing a great job with her. This kind of work you're doing here deserves wide recognition, and I may be in a position to help you. She's a different woman since she started seeing you. And I want you to do whatever needs to be done. The cost is of no concern."

When Al was asked about his drinking, he smiled. "Of course," he said, "I drink more than I should, but I'm in the dog-eat-dog world. I can't take the time to reflect and to relax. Sure as hell someone is going to shoot me down. Anyway, I know I have to watch my drinking. I quit altogether a few years back for almost three-and-a-half years. I'm not an alcoholic."

He wanted to talk about Helen: "She's been a great girl, but she really has been kind of protected. Now she wants a job, so I'll get her one. But I still believe that a woman belongs in the home. I'll get her some typing to do at home."

He talked about the kids and wanted the therapist to talk to them as well. "They don't appreciate anything I've tried to do. They've gone to the best schools, had the best of everything, and every one of them is bright as hell. But it's a funny world. These kids don't know what the hell a war is, or a depression. Life hasn't been easy for me, but I've been tough enough to last and to do well. Hell, I never went to college at all. I was damn glad to get through high school. But I made it because I didn't quit. You know, Doc, I like you!"

When Helen finally divorced him, Al became a complete alcoholic. He was forced to sell his business, and seemed to be a sad and broken man. He needed Helen, and she wanted to be his wife, but she couldn't do it for him, and he was unable to admit his need. His drinking reflected how heavily the master role wore on him. And when he could no longer be the master to his family, when his role at work as supereminent master was threatened, he began to disintegrate. Al will probably die before he agrees to do something about himself. As he stood up to leave on his last visit, his eyes were sad and bloodshot. He had taken a couple of drinks before his appointment, his mouth was drawn, his coat wrinkled, and he looked much older than ever before. He put his hand on the therapist's shoulder and said: "This is a good thing you've got here. When you want to go public, let me know. And take good care of Helen. She's a good girl. If you need any help, just call me. I'll be here."

Don had married a Mexican girl, Bonita, whom he had met in a restaurant where she worked as a waitress. She was a beautiful woman, responsive and warm, attentive and devoted to him and the three children. At the time of their marriage, Don, a Korean veteran, was trying to finish school in accounting. Bonita had agreed to work and continued her job until the final two weeks of pregnancy. After the baby was born, she invited her mother to live with them for a time so that she could continue to work. Don had always been a shy person, was heavy-set with thick glasses, and had never been very successful with women. He was terribly afraid of them. They had been married in the Catholic Church; Don was converted, much to Bonita's joy, but had refused to attend Mass shortly after the wedding. She had continued to go alone.

Bonita never questioned his judgment, permitted him to make all the decisions about home and furnishings, accepted his political views, cooked whatever he liked, kept meals waiting for him at all hours, and constantly acceded to his every wish. When Don became a successful CPA, he began to feel a new pressure in the relationship. He was an important man and was expected to have some kind of social life. He was a partner in an important firm and began to make good money. Women that had ignored him continually before began to pay attention to him. His confidence in himself seemed to grow, and he established a reputation as a witty, interesting companion. When he attended social functions with increasing regularity, he found that Bonita didn't fit in. He was ashamed of her. She couldn't talk about anything. Gradually he began excluding her from his social life. She never complained. When he asked her to go, she was ready. When he ignored her, she was docile and compliant.

He began having an affair with one of the secretaries at work and gradually became more open about it. Bonita never suspected. She recognized that their sex life was not as good as it had been, but she attributed that to Don's increasing age and the pressure of work. At first she had refused to take the pill after the third child was born, but finally had given into Don's argument: "Well, if the damn Pope wants to support my kids and send them to college, let his boys come over here and tell me about it. He's not going to run my family." Bonita gave in, but still sex was intermittent and perfunctory. She could feel Don's indifference but had learned not to question her master. She began to see evidence on his clothes that he had been in the company of other women, but she never mentioned it to him. She probably would never have gone for help if Don's mistress had not pressured him to get a divorce and marry her because she was tired of her role at parties as the other woman.

Actually Don brought Bonita for counseling to make it easier for her to accept the divorce. Even in this circumstance she was passive and docile. She simply wanted to be assured that she would not lose the children. "If he doesn't love me any more, I guess he will have to find someone else." The tears flowed freely and copiously, but always with dignity. Bonita was a beautiful woman, sensuous and trusting, warm and genuine. She conversed extremely well, and after the initial nervousness of the first interview, she revealed a great deal of depth, sensitivity and common sense. She merely needed to know that she was accepted. She had learned much from Don, and she was grateful. He had taught her many things about the American way of life. She had read widely at his suggestion, was reasonably well-informed about American politics and literature, had enjoyed a number of movies and had a good understanding and evaluation of them. She recalled the many wonderful times she had enjoyed with Don before he had made a lot of money.

Don was not able to appreciate Bonita's true beauty. Once her docility was flattering to him, her openness, her willingness to try anything. But gradually he had cut her off and left her to her own resources. She had absorbed herself in the children. He was desperately unsure of himself in his new social arena, and his dissatisfaction with his wife was largely a projection of his own insecurity in his new environment. The secretary with whom he fell in love had made him more comfortable in the unfamiliar cliché of socializing. Don had no deep relationships with anyone. He did not come off as a master in his social contacts, but as a garrulous, witty, successful CPA.

They agreed on a "creative separation" for six months without having recourse to lawyers. During the time of separation, Bonita began to blossom out. She discovered that she was marvelously talented as an artist. She began taking some classes in an adult education course at the university. She joined a Spanish-speaking club and actually participated in a show produced for educational television. She was offered a job on the staff to teach Spanish on television to children. The program fell through after thirteen weeks, but she gained a great deal of confidence and experience. Near the end of the separation, Don began seeing her regularly. His relationship with the secretary was difficult. She was expensive and insensitive. She was often interested in other men at parties and was effusive in showing them her affection. When Don complained, she insisted that she was not married to him and that she had to look out for herself. Or she accused him of being unreasonably jealous and demanding. On two occasions, he left parties in anger when she was, according to him, "making a play for some other man."

Under the pressure of the new relationship, Don entered into therapy with honest effort. In a group program he began to recognize his own insecurity and the efforts he made to compensate for it. He recognized his own fear of his father and the deep dependency that he had developed upon his mother. He made a reasonably successful effort to deal with his father as a real person and not as the ogre that he had considered him to be in childhood. He recognized how his mother had manipulated him for her own interests. Gradually, he began to recognize his fear of expressing love and realized that he played the role of master. Soon he wanted to move back in with Bonita, but she resisted. Don felt this impossible to take. Bonita had become interested in one of the members of her art class and enjoyed exploring the possibilities of her new relationship. For the first time in her life, since childhood, she was able to express anger and resistance. She had resented the role of servant, but her own insecurity had permitted her to play it well. She respected Don as the father of her children, an extremely important issue with her, and finally agreed to date him at intervals. Don found her more interesting than any other woman he had ever known. His own need to be a master had changed, and he began to recognize his own longing for an honest, close warm relationship. After about seven months, Bonita agreed to live with

Don again. Both continued in a group program and are still in it, and the marriage seems sound and creative.

The master/servant relationship often holds up very well. The children, however, usually grow very dependent upon their mother and have no relationship with their father at all. When the children are raised, the master/servant relationship is a very lonely one indeed. In reality, they have no relationship, only a kind of structured arrangement. At first sight, the master seems to be the bad guy and the servant the innocent victim. But in reality, each of them derives something supportive from his role. The servant can give in to her passivity, is not required to face her insecurity, and does not know how to express her anger. She can appear to be successful and "feminine" when she is only childish and often quite dull as a person. Her life has centered in the little details of life, and her conversation is sparkling with homely anecdotes which are often quite boring and inconsequential. To be trapped at a party with a servant can be excruciating, unless she happens to be a good listener — which fortunately she often is. But she does not really have to be in touch with herself as a person. Her whole existence centers around her man who gives artificial strength and meaning to her life.

The master and his servant frequently become deeply depressed when the children are gone. They have nothing to talk about, nothing really to share. Often the master can mellow. In reality, his synthetic anger becomes pointless. His true tenderness comes to the fore. He is not as important as he was in business, and there are fewer employees and no children to order around. His anger is diminished. He begins to recognize his need of other people, his need to love rather than to be angry. Once he did not concern himself about this, since it was all part of his act; but now he is lonely and afraid. He can show great affection for grandchildren when he was unable to show the least sign of warmth to his own children. He seems to have mellowed, and has given in to the tenderness and softness already present.

And the servant can change as well. When the children are gone, it helps if she is able to be the attentive grandmother. And when she is no longer needed to meet the perfunctory and well-disciplined demands of her aging master, perhaps they will drive to Florida, or enjoy each other in Bermuda or Hawaii. They will do the things they planned on doing, they will go to the places they wanted to go, they will do the things they hoped to do.

Nate and Ardith raised six children when Nate was a fearsome tyrant and Ardith moved to his least gesture. If she were watching television for a little while in the afternoon while getting dinner, she would jump to her feet and busy herself when she heard him open the back door. He came home when he pleased, was gone when he pleased, grumbled if the meals were not just right, complained if there was a trifle too much

starch in the shirts, insisted that she press his shorts
and T-shirts. If she played bridge one afternoon a
week, she made certain that he was home in plenty of
time to serve.

The children are all successful in their careers. The
younger ones, who did not really know their father in
his more tyrannical days, are warmer and less inhib-
ited. Their guilt is not so overpowering. But even they,
like the older children, could only laugh behind his
back. They never dared challenge him. He was the
master. One word from him and they did better in
their school work. They dated according to his sched-
ule, and learned to get around him only by stealth and
complex planning. They became adept at lying, lest
they face the full power of his anger. They never questioned their chores at home; they never approached
him for permission. Nor did they ever know him until
recent years. They were not permitted to have an
opinion until they were married. And yet, most of
them married well.

Now Nate and Ardith are alone, but somehow they
learned to find a new rhythm and balance in their relationship. Much leisure time is spent watching the television programs that they like, and Ardith gets up
regularly to provide him with coffee or a snack. When
he talks about her now publicly to friends, as he often
does, he speaks of her with tenderness and warmth.
She, too, has grown intellectually and attends extension courses at the university. She is becoming her own

person and is no longer the docile servant. Nate, too, in his own fumbling way, can now bring her hot cholo-late and cookies when she is tired. Master and servant are becoming mutually assertive lovers at long last.

Our research reveals that the rigid master needs desperately to feel superior, to receive attention, to be listened to. Ofter he feels that he has been called to a "God-given" work that he does uniquely. The servant doesn't argue with the master about politics, of course, or even about plumbing or the color of the living room carpet. He knows it all. Often, too, he is one of the "locker room boys," "an old jock," who prefers the company of men to a group of "stupid women." He regards women as "less" — less intelligent, less interesting, less energetic.

The rigid servant girl is the breeder of children, the super-housewife, the governess. It is wrong to leave the children, to be away when they come home from school, to be careless in the attention paid to clothes or housework or meals. Sexually she is usually docile and unimaginative. She would only initiate sex if the master told her to on certain occasions. Usually she would be mechanical and simply want to please the master. Often sex is not important to her.

The master usually has strong power needs and often lives a cultured life with books, records, plays, music, the country club, important luncheons with exciting people. He admires success in any field. He is demanding to his children, but rarely has any genuine kind of relationship with them. Behind his arrogance there is a dependence upon the strong, overpowering mother. Servant wives are often older than their husbands and feel fortunate to have landed them. The children are usually afraid to disappoint the master, who wants them to be carbon copies of himself. When such children begin acting out, there is usually no stopping them.

The servant wife lacks identity and projects her powers onto the master in idolatrous love. She often quotes him interminably. He is the possessor of all that is worthwhile. He is the great teacher of all — culture, sex, whatever. Often the servant girl was the child of a master type of father whom she tried unsuccessfully to please.

The master/servant relationship bears some semblance to the daddy/doll relationship but differs in two important ways:

(1) The master expects and demands more service, the daddy is more protective and nurturant.

(2) Servants are immeasurably more capable than dolls. They help when their husbands' covert dependence and weakness becomes evident. They permit their masters to continue to be strong, thereby fulfilling their own need as well as the masters'.

The master/servant relationship often involves the therapist himself when he accepts great external support from his helping role. This is expecially true when he is established as a guru and surrounds himself with a small congregation of needing individuals. His word becomes "God's" word, his acceptance proof of personal worth. The client cannot do enough for him. Of course, the therapist often recognizes the manipulative quality of this relationship and hopefully moves beyond it. It would seem that the psychoanalytic framework would singularly lend itself to the master/servant relationship because it has the kind of religious structure and aura that is required and demands the absolute faith that a master expects.

Usually the master is deeply dedicated to his work, and his friendships often have much to do with his success in his chosen field. The master rarely lets down, since no amount of success is enough. The politician often typifies the master, although the politician is also often suited for the daddy/doll relationship.

We do not wish to declare the master/servant relationship unsuccesful, any more than we do the other relationships we have described. For some individuals, it seems to work and to provide meaning in life. When the master/servant relationship no longer is effective, when a man and woman involved in such a relationship recognize that it is unreal for them in their search for personal maturity and fulfillment, then each must begin the long and often painful process of experiencing his own identity. As shown in Figure 1, the master has exaggerated his controlling anger but he can learn to express affectionate love. He has been the omnipotent potter who molds the servant like clay and denies his own vulnerability. The servant must learn to express his own vulnerability. The servant must learn to express her anger so that her love will not be fawning and servile.

It is a beautiful thing to see a master become a man, a warm and loving one, who can grow truly strong when he begins to reveal his tenderness and to recognize his needs. It is also beautiful to see frightened, passive, manipulating servant girl emerge as a warm, assertive, sensitive woman strong enough to grow in becoming herself. Currently, our culture provides a somewhat better climate than in the past for a master and a servant to become not only a man and his wife, but a man and a woman. Then service is not offered out of fear and passivity, but out of affectionate love. And mastery is not a frightened man trying to prove himself, but a loving man, a secure one, being himself. Then there is no servant and master, but there are two persons who each are *mutually educating* and growing rhythmically to become alternately teacher and student.

Part Four

Independence

Chapter 8

The Confronting Relationship: Hawks

Millions of men and women saw the movie version of Edward Albee's play, *Who's Afraid of Virginia Woolf?* starring Richard Burton and Elizabeth Taylor as George and Martha, an aging professor and his childless wife. For great numbers of people it was more than an evening's entertainment; it was a powerful picture of their own relationships.

George and Martha knew how to hurt each other. They knew each button that needed to be pushed. They knew one another's weaknesses, frustration, dreams, fantasy. And they fought to kill. Yet, there was a certain longing for love that on rare moments they had known. An outsider might not know that the

189

fierceness of their struggle was a measure of the fierceness of their longing for one another. They wanted to "get" each other because they did not really have each other. Their life together was an endless competition, and to inflict pain on each other was a futile kind of outlet for the personal pain which each endured in the relationship of hawks. As shown in Figure 1, the unconscious pattern involved in a hawk relationship is the need to be on top. Hawks are fierce competitors and the energy of competition comes from their own denial of weakness or tenderness. They fight with words, they struggle for status, they strive to prove superiority. Sex is a contest, life is a chess game. They ridicule and taunt, test and prove, scream and criticize. They blame their partners for what is missing in themselves. Each day is another contest in which the competition of the preceding day is still unresolved. *When love leaves, competition arrives.*

Most of us learned from an early age that our value as persons was determined by our success in combat with others. We were compared unfavorably to a more talented brother or sister in the hopes that we would strive with greater intensity to win a parent's love. If there were no sibling to goad us to greater heights of performance, there was undoubtedly some child in the neighborhood who became a gauge of our success. We knew what would make our parents proud. We did not know that our very effort to please them was the beginning of our own undoing as integrated and secure persons. In effect, we learned that our own being was not enough, that we had to strive for excellence, that we had to struggle to be better than someone else. Unknowingly, we were being trained as hawks.

The competitive nature of our schooling only supplemented the contest begun at home. Our value as persons was determined by our success in earning grades. Perhaps even our seating arrangement was decided by our scholastic average. It was important to be popular, to be helpful, to volunteer, to be quick with the answer, to study hard, to be strong, to win. It was not important for us to enjoy our work, to love learning, to stimulate curiosity, to explore our own appetites and interests. It was important to be the best, and in such an atmosphere other people got in our way. It was wrong to hate our opponents, it was wrong even to admit that they were opponents. They were said to be our fellow classmates, but to many of us, yearning for love and acceptance, they were obstacles in our way.

Our heroes were the men and women who were successful. We read of men named Rockefeller or Kennedy who made million of dollars by aggressive competition. As boys we were expected to be athletes to test our courage. Our fathers were proud when we made the team, they encouraged us, berated us for mistakes, smiled when we did well. A girl could fight to become a cheerleader, could hope to be invited to the most important social functions, could strive to be popular with classmates and teachers alike. Parents could live out their own competitive frustrations by cheering for their children. It was as if life had given them another chance. All the neglect and loneliness of their own childhood, the emptiness and pain, could be resolved in the success of their children. For a child not to compete in some important arena was evidence of bad health, intellectual dullness, or more often, a lack of courage.

Even dating and courtship became competitive. A girl was taught to marry a man with background and promise, and a man was taught to marry a girl who would represent him well with efficiency, talent, and physical beauty. She must learn to take an interest in his enthusiasms — even if she had to be dishonest. He must be polite and considerate, interested in her conversation no matter how she bored him. Challenge was the name of the game, competition was the motive force and the power of life.

In such a world the hawks are geared for battle. The most competitive people are usually the most insecure. They are the hungriest for approval and love but substitute competition instead. Soon enough they learn that successive victories do not satisfy. They feel the emptiness underneath their quest for a feeling of personal worth. But they do not know what to do. So they continue to compete. And the American way of life encourages their competition. Men are needed to be managers and salesmen, to build cities and create new products, to promote, to seduce, to accept challenges in business, to work long hours and to make large salaries to prove their worth. Women must gain social prestige, direct clubs, spend the money their competing husbands earn. Sometimes they must challenge men in the market place. Together men and women must build bigger and more elaborate homes to hide personal emptiness. Their neighborhood becomes a measure of their worth. They struggle to buy the clothes which promise to cover a deep, personal nakedness, they purchase the endless chain of products which offer freedom and life. They will vacation in the right place, drive the right kind of car, fight for recognition, and send their children to prestigious schools. They will live eternally with fear, awaken each morning with a new set of butterflies in their stomachs, dread advancing age which announces their failure to meet their goals. Nothing is ever enough; each seeming satisfaction only provides comfort for a time. Tomorrow will come when liquor or the stock market will not make them laugh as contentedly. But to the very end, long after beauty and business acumen has disappeared, the hawks can still compete with one another, demanding in hostile artifice and symbol, the love that they dare not ask in honesty, the love and weakness that they are most likely powerless to express.

Hawks, in their way, are potentially closer to a rhythmic relationship than the dependent and often passive couples described in Part III. We have classified them as independent because, in a sense, they avoid each other, But at least they fight, and they fight with one another. They attempt to make contact. They are not satisfied to go their separate ways, to live as strangers. They want each other's love, and they want it desperately enough to do battle for it. Usually, like George and Martha, they fight destructively and with hostility. But there is hope for them if they can learn to replace hostility with anger, since the latter is always mixed with love, while the former is destructive and disintegrative. They can make their confrontation of one another more direct and honest, to appreciate their differences as persons. At the same time, there is nothing more destructive of a relationship than competition. It is never satisfied. The hawks more easily destroy each other because the wounds remain open and fresh. Their competitive struggle leads nowhere, unless they discover that they are fighting because they care. Then, anger can be hopeful.

The open anger of the hawks is hopeful because there is real contact. It is simply not real enough. There is real feeling as well, but it is often clouded so that pain and hurt comes out as anger or even rage. Hawks prod and bully, threaten and order, criticize and judge, connive and calculate. But they do not run away from each other, they do not bury themselves in work or hobbies, they do not seethe silently and alone. They threaten and humiliate, explode and attack, struggle with words and sometimes with hands and legs. But they are alive and fighting outrageously — and where there is fight, there is hope.

The angry hawks can hurt each other because they are still involved. One can predict that beneath their anger lies the potential of a relationship. Experience and research shows that it often happens that way. Maybe the hawks will ultimately tire of fighting, withdraw and go their separate ways, or become indifferent, terminating their marriage in divorce. Or maybe they will continue to endure pain, because they still care, because they still want each other. But if they are to have a rhythmic relationship, if they are to come together as persons, they must learn to fight creatively. They must begin to understand that their anger represents personal need. Indifference is symptomatic of a dead relationship.

John and Maureen are hawks. They have been fighting for almost seven years of marriage. Their worst fights occur when both are drinking. Often they fight in public. Many times they have left social engagements in a rage. John came to see me after a particularly hostile battle. He had blackened Maureen's eyes and she had cut his lip with an ash tray and scratched his face quite noticeably. Neighbors had called the police.

It was difficult for him to describe the fight. They had entertained a few couples at home. Maureen had been upset with John because he had been working long hours at his medical practice. They had argued while waiting for the guests.

"I don't think we have enough scotch," Maureen said impatiently. "That's your department, go get some."

"How much do we have?" he asked quietly.

"Take a look. Jesus, I've got my hands full," she said.

"That should be enough. Chet drinks gin anyway." He continued to read the paper and to glance at a basketball game on television.

"Well, make sure we've got enough ice," Maureen said angrily. "You run out every time we have a party."

He threw the paper down. "For Christ's sake, why do you have to turn a party into a battle? I'll get the damned ice."

He went out and returned in about ten minutes. He opened the freezer and threw the ice in. "There, Mother, is there anything else you want to fight about?"

Maureen said nothing. She moved quickly and frantically around the kitchen.

John caught the hint. "What do you want me to do?"

She smiled at him caustically: "I'd like you to get your prick up sometimes and be able to screw me. I feel like a nun."

"I'll screw you when I don't have to figure out your combination. I'm tired of your little games. Besides, who needs you. I can get sex whenever I want it."

"You probably do," said Maureen.

"Well, I might just as well. You think it anyway. I should tell you that I've got this little nurse on the side. She really digs me."

"That's about your speed. She's probably in awe of you." (She pauses.) More quietly: "Maybe that is what you need. You can't handle a woman."

"A woman! Jesus, a woman! Where the hell is the woman?"

"You son of a bitch," she said, fighting to keep back the tears. "You dirty son of a bitch. You really know how to spoil someone's evening."

"Now make me feel guilty. I ruined your evening. Christ, you've ruined a hundred of mine. You've been fighting me for a solid month. Maybe we ought to adopt a kid so you could get off my back."

"That's dirty," she said, "that's real dirty. You know damn well I wanted kids. If you had any balls, I'd get pregnant."

"What the hell do I want you to get pregnant for? That'll just mean child support." He grinned. "Then you could be the long-suffering wife and mother without a man around. There'd be plenty of guys on hand for a one-night-stand and a free meal."

"It'd be a lot better than it is. I wouldn't have some shitty doctor coming around, the hero to all of his patients. I wish the patients could see you around here. They wouldn't think you were so kind and considerate. Those fawning women ought to marry you for a few months. They'd find out what a bastard you are."

"Why don't you tell 'em. You tell all your friends anyway. Put it in the paper. John Hastings is a bastard!" He laughed and freshed his drink.

"You could mix me a drink while you're at it," she said.

"I didn't want you to get drunk before dinner. You cook a little better when you're sober."

"Well, why don't you just tell me all evening long when I can have a drink. I'll tap you on the shoulder and ask Daddy if it's okay. Then it'll be just like your practice. I'll do whatever you tell me. Too bad you didn't go out and get a real job where people don't treat you like God. I'll fix my own goddamn drink." She mixes a larger one than usual and splashes it on the ice.

"God, at that rate, we will need more scotch," he said. "You really are a slob."

"Get off my back," she said. Then she threw the drink at him. "Get out of here you bastard. We won't even have a party. They're your friends, we'll just tell them to get the hell out of here. I'm not in any mood for a party." She went to the bedroom, returned with a sweater on, mixed herself another drink, picked up her keys, and walked out the door. "See you around, big shot!" she said.

He followed her to the door. "You dirty bitch. I

suppose this really proves something. Get your ass back in here."

"Up yours," she said.

Shortly after Maureen left the guests came: Chet and Doreen, Ted and Chris. Chet was John's associate in a medical office. Ted was a possible referral source that Chet and John had begun to cultivate. The two couples arrived together in Chet's car.

They came in and sat down, admiring the house and the art objects scattered around. "What does anyone want to drink?" asked John. They gave their preferences and John brought the drinks in on a tray.

"Where's Maureen?" asked Chet.

"Well, we had a little argument," said John with a grin. "She'll be back when she cools off. But don't say I said so. Let's say she had to run an errand."

After a while. Doreen and Chris finished the salad and John began charcoaling steaks on the patio. They had just begun to eat when Maureen came in. She went to the kitchen, poured herself another drink and joined them on the patio. She had only met Ted and Chris once before. "Good to see you two again," she said. "Hi, Doreen." Then she embraced Chester fondly. "Chet, so good to see you." She sat on his lap and fondled his hair and cheeks. Then she kissed him passionately on the neck.

"Hey, Maureen," he said with an embarrassed laugh, "that's quite a greeting."

"I'll save the rest for later!" she said seductively.

John was feeling his drinks. "You won't get much, Chet," he said coldly. "It looks good, but it's kind of dead."

"Aren't we all?" Chet said appeasingly.

Doreen intervened: "The steaks are great, John."

"Yeh, he really cooks well," said Maureen. "He's so skillful. John can do anything. One of these days he'll get pregnant."

The conversation became more impersonal. Ted and Chris tried harder when they knew what they were up against. They finished the meal and went into the den to have coffee. The girls worked in the kitchen for a few minutes and then rejoined the men.

"I think we're better off with Medicare than we ever were," said Ted. "I must confess I was one of the strongest opponents."

"Everything will go socialized," said Chet. "It's that kind of a world."

"It's almost there already. What the hell's the difference, insurance or socialized medicine?"

"I think there's a big difference," said Ted. "It's not the government."

"No, it's just big business, the government's first cousin," said John.

"Don't argue with John, Ted," said Maureen. "He's an authority on everything. Especially women."

John ignored her as the conversation continued. After a few minutes Maureen said: "I want to show you something outside, Chet."

"Outside?" asked Chet.

"C'mon, I won't hurt you." They went out together. Maureen put her arm around him as they walked out of the room. "God, it's nice to feel a man," she said.

They stayed out several minutes. Shortly after they came in, Doreen suggested that they "call it a night." "I'm tired," she said, "and we've got to take the kids to Chet's parents' house tomorrow."

The leave-taking was brief and polite. Maureen embraced Ted: "I hope we'll see more of you," she said coyly. Then she embraced Chester passionately: "Give me a call sometime." She laughed. John shook hands politely and said: "I'm sorry we spoiled your evening. There's just no way to tame a drunk bitch." The guests left and Maureen busied herself in the kitchen, humming happily.

"Great party," she said. "I really dig Chet."

John was furious. She had won, she had succeeded in humiliating him." You really are a bitch," he shouted.

"Keep your voice down, darling," she said laughingly, "the neighbors will think you can't handle your wife."

He rushed into the kitchen. "Fuck the neighbors!" he said and slapped her.

Maureen got violent. "Keep your goddamn hands off of me," she screamed. Then she began throwing things.

John slapped her again. She threw a wet ash tray at him and cut his lip. He began slapping her again. She scratched his face. Then she began screaming. A short time later the police came and told them to end the argument or they would both land in jail. A few days later John sought help.

They were seen separately for several weeks and gradually got through their anger to their tears. There was no possibility of counseling to save the marriage; they needed individual therapy. Each had been hurt deeply, both at home and in their marriage. They separated for six months during their personal search for help and understanding.

Gradually they were able to appreciate their deeper feelings. Maureen said: "I've always felt like John's other self. Everywhere we went, people made over him, telling me what a great doctor he was, asking his opinion, implying that I was so lucky to have him. I was just his wife, nothing by myself. All of our friends were associates of his, all of our conversations centered around medicine. Half of the time I didn't know what they were talking about. I felt useless to him.

"I had never really been comfortable in our courtship, but our sex life was good and it seemed great to be marrying a doctor. I knew that I would have everything I didn't have at home. My parents were proud. I liked the way my father deferred to John. Suddenly I seemed to be his favorite daughter. I had always felt awkward and stupid before.

"When I didn't get pregnant the first few years, I felt I was letting John down. He was crazy about kids, coming as he did from a large family. I always felt inferior. To have kids became an obsession. It would give me some meaning in life. There was no reason I couldn't get pregnant. We discovered that John's sperm count was low, not too low, but low. I began to throw that up at him. Our sex life disintegrated. He seemed just to want relief, he didn't want me. When he wanted me, I thought he only wanted my body. When he didn't want me, I figured he had someone else. Our arguments became loud and brutal. I wanted to be somebody, and married to him I felt like nothing.

"I got good at hurting him after a while. I wanted to hurt him. I hurt so much myself. He seemed to be such a know-it-all. He never asked me about anything. I tried to read more, but even after I had read something, I didn't get it straight. I even lied about what I had read. I never finished college. I always felt bad about it. I really wasn't too bright. But I guess I still love him. I just think he doesn't love me. That really hurts, and that's why I get hostile."

Maureen cried for many hours. She went into intensive therapy because if there were three or four days between her appointments, she built up her whole system of defenses again and it was hard to reach her. She had been hurting for a long time. But she was determined to be a person. Gradually she realized that she didn't need John to make it. She wanted him if she could have a relationship, but she could make it by herself. She was a person in her own right. She had hidden behind John and then hated him for it. She had felt unworthy of him and asked him to assure her that she was a whole person. Her face became softer, she could express her love, her need, her hurt.

John tried equally as hard: "I don't know what happened. She was always talking about other men she had gone with and it used to irritate me. She always tried to attract other men no matter where we went. I didn't want to appear jealous, so I ignored it as often as I could. I was never very sure of myself. Maybe that's why I tried so hard. I was a skinny kid, not much of an athlete. I was always trying to prove myself. I screwed dozens of girls before I was married, maybe just to prove I could. I know I'm not very good-looking, and I always felt girls dated me because I was a doctor. I made a point of telling every girl I met that I was in medical school. Sometimes I think that's why I became a doctor, to be important. I was never very good at anything except books. I couldn't fix cars, couldn't play sports very well.

"Maureen used to take me like I was. She loved to have sex with me. She told me that I was the only one she ever had a real orgasm with. The others didn't mean much to her. She said that I could make her laugh and that made me happy. We used to laugh all the time. Then after a while, she said that I was making fun of people — she used to enjoy it. She said I was looking down my nose at others. I didn't feel I was. She used to like the way I talked to people. She said I had a great personality and could talk to anyone.

Then after we were married for a while, she began to say that I was always talking about myself or my work, that I never gave her a chance to say anything. She used to fight me for the floor. I fought back. I began to feel dull and boring just like I had felt when I was a kid. I didn't think that anyone liked to listen to me.

"I began working longer hours at my practice. I'd go to the hospital when I didn't have to go. And I began looking at other women. I actually had a number of brief affairs, but I still wanted Maureen. I just couldn't get her. Even if I had sex with another woman, I still went home and wanted Maureen. She really turns me on. I guess I love her, but I just can't get to her anymore. She hurts me and I hurt back."

John and Maureen were hawks, struggling to know a rhythmic relationship. Each had so much capacity for warmth, for concern, for understanding. Their very sensitivity, when perverted into hostility, made them all the more successful as hawks. Hostility turned into anger and it was gradually transformed into a positive force. Their marriage was probably saved. Presently they are living together and hopefully, communicating more creatively. They are not asking each other to supply what is lacking in themselves. They are sometimes warmly, sometimes angrily, rhythmically relating, not destroying; requesting, not demanding. Each is facing his own needs as a person and trying to do something for himself. Most of all they can admit their weakness, not transform it into hate-filled words.

Our research reveals that rigid hawks attempt continuously to say to each other: "I am as good as you are." Each tries to prove his worth by asserting superiority. The very competitive nature of our culture encourages them to stay together. To fail at marriage is to lose; to attempt a divorce is to admit that the other person has won. Hawks often remain in a marriage, a la *Virginia Woolf*, to destroy the other person in order to be free from personal pain, but when they seem to win, in reality they lose. Hawkish competition is the most destructive kind; nevertheless, it can be transformed into the most honest of confrontations between people. They do not bury their anger as do doves.

Our research further shows that rigid hawks are well-versed in intimidating techniques. They are often from homes where one parent was dominant and the other played underdog. Thus, the wounded hawks often choose partners whom they hope will be different from the parent of the opposite sex. Once the honeymoon is over, they frequently discover that they have married another hawk. The courtship itself was a kind of dishonest manipulative seduction. During the "romantic period" of the courtship, each was exceedingly receptive to the wishes of the other. When the period of disillusionment comes, the competition hits with great fury. Our preliminary research shows that it is not at all unusual for the husband in such a relationship to have an affair with a more docile and receptive woman. Increasingly, our culture permits the same option to a woman.

Often enough the competitive battle can be sustaining and exciting. The hawks lose their appetite for love, and sex becomes an occasional manipulation, sometimes exciting after a hostile battle. But even sex is not a giving in, it is only a temporary relief. Competition replaces love in this power-play relationship. It is what one writer has called "symmetrical escalation."

Hawks may even grow to respect each other as opponents, but they seem incapable of loving each other as friends. Each remains ultimately alone and unloved. They fight for love but do not receive it. The pain of being unloved is the most acute known to man. Such pain can be a powerful force for competition and meeting challenges. But no victory is ever enough, because no victory makes contact with the center of the person. It is always a symbolic victory, a vain attempt to prove that the hawk is truly worthwhile. The deep pain continues to provide energy to fight, moving the hawk to inflict pain on another, especially on the one other who threatens his or her area of seeming strength.

Hawks aim for the jugular and turn the domestic scene into all-out war. Competition is unceasing. It is active, high-level competition, the contest of a top dog and top cat fighting for dominance. Without help, they will battle to the end, struggling to prove with each short-lived victory that they are worthy of love

— yet never really believing it. Tomorrow there will be another skirmish, another hill to climb, another sniper to kill.

As Figure 1 shows, the male hawk is either a master or a daddy or a combination of both. The female is a mother or bitch, or partly each. The hawks look beyond each other in their warfare and see only themselves. The master may still be telling his own mother to cease controlling him, pleading with her to love him. A bitch may well be fighting the father who ruled with an iron hand. All the energies of the relationship are directed towards a pyrrhic victory. There well may be moments of peace but never enough security for love. Hawks know ultimately and radically that they are not loveable. The best they can hope for is a temporary truce or transient satisfaction.

The hawk in therapy needs strong and consistent help. He or she may well divorce and marry a pushover like the servant or son, but such a relationship may soon grow dull and meaningless. The hawk needs a challenge, and perhaps the only worthwhile challenge is to become a person. The hawk wants a real relationship, and the very fury of his assault is a gauge of how badly he wants it. Even in therapy he may compete to be the best patient before he settles down to become a person. It takes a good and insightful therapist to resist his manipulation. He is often disciplined, usually energetic, alive, determined to win. Therapy itself can become a part of his game, giving him better tools to manipulate his environment. He will learn to say the right words, feign the right emotion, practice to win the admiration of his "group" — so desperately does he want love and approval.

It is probably useless to attempt "marriage counseling" with most couples, but more especially with hawks. Their very hostility with a spouse indicates their demand that the spouse do something for them that they must do themselves. They must experience the deep hurt of being unloved. They well may emerge from therapy as different persons, aware of their weaknesses, hurts, and vulnerability which will give them the rhythm of being human. They will have learned the important lesson that *whenever you win, you lose*. Winning and losing are but human constructs in which winners always pay a price.

With hawks in particular, to win a battle is often to lose the war, because they fight with blind *hostility* rather than with a productive kind of *anger*. Hostility flows from a deep, personal turmoil and only apparently has any real connection with the circumstance which seems to trigger it. It is stored up anger, or anger with amnesia, and its origin lies deep within the psyche. It hides a painful, personal hurt, unconsciously felt, and only when the deep hurt is expressed can the hawks begin to know a rhythmic relationship.

The hostility of the hawks is a desperate camouflage, a smoke screen which hides the pain and "weakness" which they have never permitted themselves to reveal.

Only when they move beyond hostility can their anger have objectivity and balance. Only then will their anger serve to ward off hurt in the present. Hostility is directed to the past and is in reality a muffled and unacknowledged cry of deep pain.

If the hawk can feel his hurt and go to the core of his personal aloneness, he may emerge as one who acknowledges his need for love and his longing to give it. He will not have to hide behind symbols of strength which will never satisfy, which only increase his insatiable appetite. He may have to experience once again the loneliness of a childhood when he was never loved, only praised for a command performance. He will undoubtedly shed the copious tears of hurt, cry deep and heart-rending cries. He may have to live through the desperation and pressure of his childhood; he may have to feel the hurts which he denied or transformed into accomplishments. He will admit his weakness, his fear of tenderness, and the tension which only hide his ever-present pain.

But the quest is worth the struggle. He will feel his body again, he will know the freedom to decide what he wants to do, to decide what challenges he wants to accept. He will not live with the compulsiveness which gave today meaning only in terms of tomorrow. He will slow down, learn to enjoy, learn to stop punishing himself for a crime he never committed. He will feel the tons of guilt lift from his back he will see his mother and father in an entirely new light. His sexual enjoyment will be something other than the anxiety which drove him, other than the pain which demanded that he prove himself. His relationship to others will be more than a mendicant's demand for approval. He will discover the depths of his continuing manipulation of everyone to find the love which he is unable to express or to accept.

And most of all, be he man or woman, the hawk will be able to relate to another, not as master or bitch, not as mother or father, but as equal person to equal person. The hawk can know what it is to be free enough to love, strong enough and weak enough to be loved. Life will not be a continuing contest, an eternal and impossible proof of worth. It will be a mutually comforting relationship where each can be a complete person to the other.

Chapter 9

The Accommodating Relationship: Doves

C. S. Lewis, in his classic *Screwtape Letters,* writes tellingly of the dove relationship, insisting that a young couple, intent on destroying each other, need only be convinced that they should spend a lifetime struggling to please each other.

Dave Martin stepped into the bathroom to shave. For the fourth consecutive morning there were dirty diapers in the toilet bowl. He was nauseated. "Donna!" he called.

"Yes, darling, I'm just getting your orange juice." She walked into the bathroom, her negligee subtly tied loosely in front. She put the orange juice down on the shelf next to the sink, approached him coyly and asked, "What do you want, darling?" The dove-ing had begun!

He was angry but he grinned. She brushed against him. He put his arms around her and began to get aroused.

"Do you want something?" she asked.

Dave was disarmed. He had wanted "something" last night in bed but felt too guilty to ask directly. Donna had sensed his feeling and chatted until she had dissipated his ardor. She often talked away his feelings. When she had finally stopped talking, he had made a motion towards her. She had said, "I'm really tired, but I'd like to please you."

"No," he had said. "You've had a tough day. We'll save it, it'll just get better."

"I'm lucky to have you," she had said. "You're always considerate. I guess that's what I love about you the most." She had cuddled against him like a little girl. He had wanted to move his leg but he did not want to be inconsiderate. He had continued to lie in an uncomfortable position. But sleep was impossible so he turned over on his side." You're restless, darling," she had said kindly. "What's wrong?"

"Nothing. I just wanted to turn over on my side."

"Don't you like me touching you?"

Actually he didn't, but he had never been able to tell her. He had heard her tell her girlfriend, Eloise, how nice it was to be married to a man who liked to cuddle.

Finally they had gone to sleep and Donna had won another gentle battle without acknowledging a war.

Now the morning after, the silent struggle began again. He held her and fondled her in the bathroom. He did not want to offend her, and although he was in a hurry to shave and to get to work, he did not assert himself. "There's no time now, silly boy," she said, "besides I need to feed you! Do you have time to eat?" she asked. She always asked. It had to be a special request. He was irritated, but he did not reveal it.

"Do you have anything ready?" he asked. He knew that she didn't.

"No," she replied, "but it will only take a minute."

He knew that it would take twenty minutes. "No, really, darling, I'll just drink the orange juice and get some coffee and a roll at the office."

"I wish you'd let me," she said.

"No, darling, you can do it tomorrow. Actually, I like to eat something every morning before I leave."

She was ready for him. "I thought you were going to lose a little weight," she said.

"Well, maybe I should, but I do enjoy breakfast." He said it kindly; he had said it a dozen times before.

She touched him casually and patted his stomach: "I like your little fat tummy."

An impulsive thought flashed into his head: "Then why the hell do we have sex so seldom?" But he didn't say it — in the passive tradition of the doves. He would say it another way, kindly, but he would say it. And she would respond, kindly, but she would respond. And nothing would change. It was a silent war.

He began sipping his orange juice. She noticed the diapers. "Oh, I forgot about those. I'll get them out of your way. I was just too tired last night. I know you don't like to pick them up." She had given her signal and he responded.

"No, no, I don't mind," he said, dropping his orange juice and taking the dripping diapers from the bowl.

"Oh thank you darling! Say, if you get a chance, will you take my green suit to the cleaners? But if you're too busy, I can wear something else for the party. It's just that they give you better service than they do me."

The message was clear again and he took her green suit from the closet and put it on the bed. He acceded to another passive command.

She cuddled against him like a little girl. He held her for a few moments, waiting for a chance to get away and finish shaving. Finally he pulled back.

"Hold me just a little longer, darling," she said. "I know you have to go."

He held her. The pressure in his stomach increased. He wanted to break away. "Let's make love!" he said.

"Oh, you don't have time, darling."

His stomach tensed again. He patted her gently and pulled back with a kind smile: "Okay, darling, but tonight when I get home, we'll have a martini and make love on the living room floor."

But he really knew that tonight it would be something else. There would be the baby to take care of, or dinner to get on. He would be in no hurry, but she would tell him that he was, that she shouldn't delay his evening meal. He would help her and she would tell him to relax. When he relaxed, she would ask him kindly to help her for a moment. Then they would eat and she would be tired and it would begin again — the silent war.

Dave and Donna are the doves at work making a marriage succeed. On the surface they appear to be the opposite of the hawks, but in reality their very power lies in their subtlety. Their relationship, like that of the hawks, is an independent one since they avoid each other and fight for control by a "weakness" which is passive strength. They know they must never admit to their ability to control by their plea of helplessness. Their fights are the most subtle of all because they do not even admit to being adversaries. They fight with niceness and kindness. They have an intransigent rule: never to permit anger or violence, hostile words or impulsive put-downs. They compete passively, fight quietly, camouflage their anger in tense controls and silence. They are not hawks, they are the gentle doves who battle with saccharine sweetness.

Doves will not admit to competition nor even to fighting. The secret of their control is in their absolute passivity. Doves are not the top dog and top cat as are hawks, they are the hound dog and pole cat. They are

Dave and Donna, a doll competing with a nice guy. They can also be a son and servant, a doll and a son, or the servant and the nice guy. But they win everything by being nothing. They win by withdrawing from the competition and patronizingly dismissing those who give way to aggression.

Doves are passive manipulators. They manipulate by making their concern for the other paramount. They avoid confrontation, keep the peace at any price. Doves maintain their independence by their passivity and concern. Theirs is a secret strength but it is a genuine strength. Their helplessness (often their apparent helplessness) is their very method of control. In reality the passive doves do not need the help they apparently ask. Their very need is a way of controlling. It is a passive and silent demand which never surfaces. Actually these are independent people who feign dependence to mask their system of manipulation. Among the manipulators these are the most clever and effective of all.

Doves use guilt as one of their primary weapons. They appear as guilt-ridden and they are masters at creating guilt in others. By appearing helpless and dependent and making light of their own pain, they create a sense of obligation in others to care for them. They are the Christian caricature. Their "meekness and humbleness of heart" is their private arsenal. They turn the other cheek even as they assassinate. Their very morality creates obligation and guilt in others.

Christianity is useful to them, for its virtues can be easily distorted and manipulated. "Love" can be turned into "Look what I do for you!" The "humility" which says: "I don't want to be a bother" in reality demands absolute obedience. Their "concern" becomes an imperative that others be concerned about their needs. Even their personal guilt is a way of making others feel guilty.

It is important to understand that most of the guilt that the dove creates is in reality unexpressed hostility and resentment. The dove does not deal with such feelings. He creates guilt in others instead. Some of the guilt is real and authentic, often a recognition of a desire to grow. But the greater part is caused usually by those doves who want to be in control and who use guilt for that purpose. When the dove can admit to his hostility — which he may have to do in a therapeutic setting at first — he can find the harmony between his love and anger which is so essential in the rhythmic relationship.

Let us reconstruct what happened to Dave and Donna in therapy. In the safety of the therapeutic situation they were invited to say what they really felt rather than to play the cooing dove game. Dave said what he really wanted to say when stepped into the bathroom. Replaying the scene he said to Donna: "Get those goddamn diapers out of here. I've told you twenty times, and you tell me that you'll do it. I know you're trying to punish me, to tell me how hard it is to have a baby and to take care of him. Well, I've got the message, you've told me a thousand different ways. So who cares, you bitch. Get those damn diapers out of here right now or I'll shove them down your whining throat. And knock off this martyr shit right now."

In replaying to Dave, Donna also expressed her resentment. In therapy Donna was free to respond the way she really wanted to: "Go to hell, you big baby. You want to be waited on hand and foot. Pick up the damn diapers yourself, they won't hurt you. You wanted the kid. Why couldn't we have waited a few years to have kids? I didn't want the damn baby. Now we can't travel or do a thing. Well, I'll show you, you son of a bitch, I'll make you sick of this kid. You won't get your sex unless you start thinking of someone besides yourself. You don't know what it means to take care of a drooling kid all day long. Christ, I don't do anything any more except clean and pick up."

Then Dave answered what he really felt. "Listen, you spoiled bitch. I'm so damn sick of your passivity, I could puke. If you'd plan your goddamn day, we could get a lot of things done. What the hell do you think I do all day long? I'm so fucking sick of your little girl tricks. I've got to beg you for a piece of ass. What the hell are you punishing me for? You can get a baby sitter any time you please. You buy every damn thing you see. You don't care how I feel. You cook when you damn please, you don't realize that I'm pooped when I come home. I have to listen to all your shit. Everything you do for me, you want a merit badge. You never give me a chance to respond. You're asking for something everytime you give me something. Just get the hell out of the bathroom and get my breakfast. I don't want to hear one more time, 'Do you want breakfast?' Hurry it up. I've got to work my ass off today to support your expensive tastes."

Then Donna got down to it: "Don't order me around you weak son of a bitch. I can wrap you around my finger. I knew you were weak when I married you. You've got no balls. If you'd stand up to me once in a while, I might respect you. But you just dump your load of guilty shit on me. I've got to play this little game with you. You'd fall apart if I whistled too loud. I'm bored silly with you and your stupid job. I buy things because I feel so lousy. I don't know what the hell else to do. If I look at you cross-eyed, you pout. You don't love me, you just want someone around to mother you and to make you think you're a big man."

Then Dave responded: "You couldn't mother anyone, you bitch. I played your little game all through courtship. *Then* you couldn't get enough of me. You didn't have to sleep all the time then and, you used to work for a living. Now you just sit around on your ass and whine. Jesus, I'd like to break your neck. My stomach feels like it's always in a knot. Why the hell do I have to spend my whole life pleasing you? You're just like my goddamn mother. She was always sick and tired. You're just like her. Every damn thing I get, I

pay double for. Christ, I'd just like to take off. Even
the kid bugs the hell out of me. I gotta watch every
damn thing he does. I've gotta pay my dues every
night. Even the kid has become an anchor around my
neck. Well, I'm all through taking your sweet shit.
I'm all through begging for a little piece of your blue-
ribboned ass. Go fuck yourself, you bitch. You goddamned baby!"

Donna wasn't through: "God, you're no prize. You
just sit around here waiting for me to make a move.
I've got to plan everything. All that matters to you is
that damn job. You frightened little junior executive.
You go through life kissing everyone's ass. I can't raise
my voice without you falling apart. You've always got
to know 'What's wrong?' You're wrong, that what's
wrong. This isn't a marriage, it's a goddamned ping-
pong game. So you just keep bribing me. Take me on
another trip, or buy me another house, or let me open
another charge account. And smile sweetly. Then I'll
tell everyone what a nice husband you are, how nice
you are to me. You're so goddamned nice I can't stand
you. I'd like to slap your controlled face till the blood
comes. I'd give anything to hear something besides
that quiet voice that's always in control. Jesus, I hate
you!"

Before therapy Dave and Donna as good doves
would never fight like this. They felt they had no
"right" to be hostile. They had held their hostility inside and beat each other to death indirectly. If they

had fought like hawks, they might have had to begin the marriage or end it. Perhaps they would have accomplished nothing. But they would have turned their smouldering smiles into a frontal attack. Meanwhile they had continued to kill each other with kindness and kept careful score of everything they gave.

Doves are often the victims of a culture that has taught men and women to be polite and "nice" at any cost — even if the cost is the loss of one's own identity. At home they learned to deny their true feelings, not to talk back, not to fight with brothers and sisters, not really to tell parents the truth. Peace was more important than true feelings. They were not to quarrel or get angry. In school they were not to question teachers or to express discontent. They were expected to do meaningless assignments with the same cheerfulness as they would the helpful ones. And they were taught to "control" themselves, to be kind, docile, obedient.

Many systems of education are based on repressed emotions and unquestioned obedience. Military school takes pride in the development of controlled men. So do many parochial schools. Not only are anger and rebellion to be repressed, but other feelings as well. Honesty means telling the truth only when one is asked. When the teachers are priests or nuns, whose very office makes them "sacred" persons, the student is expected to be even more cautious of expressing genuine feeling. His very teachers are professionally "virtuous" and honest behavior often seems reprehensible in such surroundings. Many citizens extoll the effective discipline of military schools or parochial institutions. This is how little "men" and "cultured" women are made. This is also how dishonest doves are produced.

The public schools as well are responsible for controlled behavior. The very nature of the classroom in our culture — with its emphasis on order and discipline, work and regimentation, established curriculum and teaching plans, silence and sitting still — produces the passive aggression of the doves. The desirable student is most often the one who complies. The most creative individual may have to pay a penalty. The good teacher is one who can control a class. No one seems concerned about the hostility that may smoulder under such controls.

This is not to suggest that violent outbursts of hostility are a recommended practice outside of therapy. But the depths of the rage indicates how long the feelings have been "controlled." Our culture encourages such behavior. On occasion we can see it break free — when the students rebel on campuses, when men and women get behind the wheel of a car, vicariously in the voices of spectators at football games, in the rising hostility towards the police. If feelings do not have an opportunity to be expressed, men and women store up anger and spew it forth in violent outbursts. They have been instructed to deny negative feelings, to put up with bores, with unreasonable laws, with impersonal and rigid authority. Anger builds up and becomes hostility because it is considered wrong, or impolite, un-Christian or unkind. Beneath the hostility are hurt and sadness struggling for freedom. When the hostility finally comes forth, the hawks express it so violently that one can hardly endure it. The doves express it in subtle, passive aggression, so consistent and all-pervading that it creates almost permanent tension. It leaks out slowly, so slowly and so guardedly that it makes an angry response seem unwarranted. Often enough the doves do not move from the hostility to the pain which lies beneath it.

In order to move beyond hostility we must make room for anger. As we have seen, there is an important difference. Hostility is diffuse and destructive, and results from many years of suppressed natural feelings. Anger is negative caring, and when expressed at the moment it is felt, it flows out and doesn't cause deep hurt. It remains in the present to ward off harm. Hostility lives in the past and is nourished by unexpressed pain. Doves need the courage to express their anger at the moment, on a cash and carry basis, so that hostility does not build up. The distinction between hostility and anger is most important to understand.

Underneath the hostility there is hurt, and it is essential that the doves make contact with their sadness and pain.

While anger is a fighting feeling, hurt is a depressed, sad feeling, which when expressed is usually accompanied by crying, or at least moist eyes. When both anger and hurt can be expressed spontaneously, the couple is well on the way to expressing themselves rhythmically.

Thus Dave and Donna took yet another step to communicate and move beyond their blind rage. When Dave saw the diapers in the toilet bowl, he admitted: "It really hurts me when you ignore my feelings. I have tried to tell you how I feel, Donna, but you don't seem to care. You don't want to please me. I'm afraid you don't love me."

Donna then was able to admit: "I guess I'm getting even with you. You seem to work all the time, you don't have any interest in me. I don't seem like a person any more. I have to try to be sexy because that's the only way I get any attention. And when I get attention that way, I don't like myself. I really hurt. I don't even enjoy sex because I can't let myself go. I can't give to you. I can only play games and fantasize. I'm depressed and sad much of the time. I guess that's why I buy things and complain so much. I have blamed you for my feelings."

Dave then said: "I'm really afraid that I'm not making it on the job. I've been so preoccupied all the time. I keep thinking so much about the future that I can't live in the present. I guess I don't have much confidence in myself. I was never really very confident about anything. I just pretend to be because I'm afraid that someone will find out. I even hide my fear from you."

Donna then said: "I'm the same way. I keep thinking that you're going to run off with some cute secretary. I wonder how you can love me. I never finished school, I don't do anything exciting, I'm bitchy most of the time. I've just kind of let myself go downhill."

Such communication was the beginning of Dave and Donna's marriage. But countless other Daves and Donnas, fighting their passive war, may well remain doves for the entirety of their lives. They may remain afraid to take the risk of a relationship, which means to reveal one's self truly and honestly to another and to see what happens. Often enough, love is the result, but always growth. Instead, they may continue to fight like doves, perhaps denying to themselves that they are fighting, but feeling the pressure of one another's subtle stabs. Soon they might not even feel that.

Our psychological research reveals that the rigid dove relationship is one of "mutual pleasing," based on the false assumption that the best relationship can be maintained by a phony accommodation. As revealed in Figure 1, the doves do not express their anger and admit their strength. Actually they do not love each other, but they are too guilty and restrained to show their dissatisfaction outwardly. They believe in appearances but avoid close contact. They withdraw from reality into independent separate worlds. They never make a scene, they maintain affective neutrality. Such relationships develop from a distortion of the Judaeo-Christian ideal which stresses love without conflict. Each wants to be "unselfish," to do "what the other wants." Each fights the battle for the other and manages to feel blameless and used. Keeping the waters calm is central, to avoid conflict at any cost. This becomes a nothing-nothing relationship.

Another false assumption revealed in our research is that each dove feels responsible for the other party in the relationship, while neither member takes responsibility for himself. This places an additional burden of guilt on each other's shoulders, and resentment is the inevitable result. Until each member of the relationship takes responsibility for himself, the relationship remains at an impasse. Thus, until each one can become responsible for his own needs and have the courage to stand alone in the face of the other, the relationship will not have the creative conflict necessary for growth. To be real it must become a responsible-responsible relationship.

Although doves seldom seek therapeutic help as a couple — since their marriage is usually a "perfect" one made in heaven — Doug and Sandy came for help. Guiltily each blamed himself for the problem, insisting that the other party was most considerate and loveable. They came for help because Sandy had felt immense sadness and depression from which she could not seem to escape. Doug had always felt responsible, since he believed that it was his job, as a good dove in marriage, to make his partner happy. Sandy's misery, he was certain, was his fault. Sandy, on the other hand, felt continually responsible for Doug's sexual unhappiness. He did not tell her he was unhappy. She presumed it since they had not had sex with any frequency for many years. Before marriage, they had intended to have children, but when Sandy did not get pregnant in the first couple of years, they decided against a family. After ten years of marriage, they seldom slept together. They did not want to disturb one another.

Very likely Doug was as deeply depressed as Sandy. Her sadness had been her way of controlling him. He was powerless in the marriage. But so was she. Each had to live up to an image and there was no possibility of escape. Nor was there any possibility of therapy. Sandy was given a few pills by a friendly psychiatrist who sensed the futility of taking the relationship apart.

Dan and Jeanne came for help because Dan was sexually impotent. Jeanne was not sexually disinterested, but the whole approach to the sexual act had been to please her husband. She assured me that she was not interested in her own pleasure, only in satisfying him. Dan insisted that he did not want to be selfish, that he wanted to be a good husband and to satisfy his wife. She insisted that she could live without sex and that she only wanted Dan to be happy. After several thrusts of the Alphonse-Gaston routine, it became clear that Jeanne's desire only to do her duty and to please Dan had helped him to feel sexually very unappealing. When he wanted sex, he was required to make the right overtures and Jeanne assured him that she was happy to share her favors with him. Again, there was no opportunity to provide real therapy since there was no motivation on the part of the individuals. They felt that there was nothing wrong with their marriage, only something defective in Dan's ability to perform. Presumably they are still "happy" in their "perfect marriage."

The dove-like individual often comes to the therapist for help. He is usually a compulsive individual who has always wanted to please. He cannot bear the thought of hurting anyone, of incurring anyone's displeasure. He is responsible for his parents, his friends, his family, and even for the therapist. The dove can be a difficult client who manipulates the therapist as he manipulates everyone else. He is especially difficult to detect in the "love everybody" type of group therapy which has become popular in different parts of the country. He or she thinks that progress has been made because he feels greater comfort in a therapy group. More than likely he has simply learned the rules of the group and will cling to it as his new community. Nothing has really happened. He is a clever enough dove to detect what the therapist wants, what the rules are governing a group, and he behaves accordingly to be loved by one and all.

It is difficult for the dove to learn, in or out of marriage, that he is only really responsible for himself. This sounds to him like "selfishness." He has not learned the distinction between selfishness and self-love. There are advantages for him in his role of the super-responsible person. He can feel like the "good, religious" person. He can hear frequently that he is "dedicated and concerned." He can also avoid the personal challenge of being responsible for himself. He will often postpone decisions because no course of action seems acceptable, and be critical and resentful of obligations he freely assumed without acknowledging his negative feelings. He finds it hard to say "No" to anyone and will resent having said "Yes." He will insist regularly that everyone takes advantage of him, that people bleed him to death. With the next breath he will accept responsibility for the whole world.

The dove wants desperately to be loved, but will never be himself long enough to take the risk. He only shows his artificial and seemingly acceptable veneer. When he does indulge in an outburst of anger, it is short lived. He has been carefully taught that anger is unacceptable, and besides, his passive aggression is more effective and less risky. He cannot bear to have anyone at odds with him. His sudden snap of anger is only an indication of the depths of his stored-up feelings.

The doves will have their peace in marriage. They will have quiet evenings and quiet children and picnics without obvious rancor. They will have attentive service, programmed sex, kind words, and well-tailored lawns. They will have success and order, comfortable existence and few surprises. They will probably not have a divorce unless one party decides to opt for life. And the abandoned dove is a sorry bird, indeed, since he thought because he owned another person, that other had no "right" to leave. In marriage, however, the doves will know little of life and almost nothing of love. They will trade reality for peace, honesty for quiet, love for a truce.

Others will speak well of them. Friends will remark how well they get on. Society will reward them for their stability in marriage, employers will congratulate them for their lifetime of service on the same job, pastors will shake their hands and thank them for their regular contributions. Their children will probably be home for the holidays and know the same programmed dullness that they knew as youngsters. The doves will endure. They accept that life because they do not believe that it can be different, because they do not dare dream that it can be other than it is.

And sadly, they will never know the love of man and woman. They will never know the excitement of discovering another person, of revealing one's self to take the ultimate risk of rejection or love. They will not need to divorce, since in reality they have never been married. They have been independent and emotionally separated since the start. They will only know role-playing, super responsibility, absorbing guilt, a hunger for acceptance that is insatiable and constant. They are a caricature of Christianity and life, they are God reduced to ten commandments, Christ reduced to an institution, love reduced to a summer stock show.

To be doves together is perhaps the most disillusioning relationship of all. It is to play the part of love perfectly without experiencing it. Perhaps they are satisfied to accept what little of life is theirs. The alternative is painful, to be honest, to be free and responsible for one's self, to acknowledge one's anger, one's manipulation, one's poverty as a person. But it is worth the pain to become alive, to know the beginning of love, to be oneself and responsibility to accept the consequences of such courage.

An entire culture has taught a man that "he is his brother's keeper," that he is responsible for those around him. Unhappy parents imposed the guilt of their own lives on the being of their children. Guilt, like the "original sin" of Adam and Eve, is passed from generation to generation. The religions have helped, insisting that man's sins are responsible for the death of Christ, preaching that man is helpless and fragile and prone to evil.

The doves have bought the whole cultural brainwash. They weep for the parents they have unwillingly hurt, for the children they inadvertently wounded, for the spouse they cannot provide with meaning and joy. In reality they should weep for themselves. They are the tragic ones, continuing to pay a debt they never incurred, fighting to give what they do not have. They must be rid of the guilt which binds them, to know the responsible love which will set them free.

Man is not his brother's keeper: his brother can keep himself. He is his brother's friend, or his brother's brother; he is only himself. He can choose to love where he will, choose to give to whom he wants, to be what he wants. Only then will he be free from guilt and artificial responsibility. Only then can he do his own thing and permit another to do his own thing as well. He owes no man anything. To be free enough to give love to another is not a debt, but a joy. No man can make it a debt. Otherwise it becomes the guilty commandment of the institution. Love is a free gift. No one can command it. And when it is given — beyond guilt, beyond compulsion, beyond fear — then the relationship of trembling doves can become a combination of mutual accommodation and creative confrontation.

Part Five

Interdependence

Chapter 10

The Rhythmic Relationship

Once in infancy we were all naturally rhythmic in our spontaneous response to life. Like the ebb and flow of the tides and the revolving motion of the seasons, our very being innately reflected this inner rhythm. We were able to be strong and weak, to cry when we were hurt, to weep when we were afraid, to laugh with our whole body when we were pleased. We were able to feel loveable and worthwhile, warm and wanted. Our parents were there to affirm us, to tell us that our very being as persons was sufficient reason to assure us of love. Our anger was not buried and turned to guilt, our petulance and pouting did not deeply offend, our existence was not at first the fulfillment of another's neurotic need. Our dependence did not bind us in emotional chains, our independence did not leave us isolated and alone. We were feeling beings who responded with freedom and creative rhythm.

But then rigidification took place. It happened subtly and often soon. Parents and teachers took command and taught us to say "yes" to some of our responses and "no" to others. They taught us to live through their eyes, to hear through their ears, to respond through their own personal fears. Life became simplistically "good" and "bad," "right" and "wrong," "acceptable" and "unacceptable." We gave adults and even siblings the right to judge our worth, to determine our merit, to manipulate our love. And in this very devastating exchange of self for a well defined role, we lost our personality and sought constant approval from those we had given the right to define us. Our self-concept was thereby lost, and we struggled helplessly to recover it. We no longer permitted ourselves to "be" and thus denied others this ultimate and uniquely human right. The rhythm was gone.

Then perhaps we married — well schooled in the art of manipulating and transferring guilt. Our anger lay hidden, our hurt unrevealed, our very love beneath the surface and powerless to blossom forth. We were rigid men and women, afraid of the rhythm of life, afraid of risking ourselves to make love possible.

We had been hurt in life, deprived, unsupported by the all-enveloping love which could have told us that it was right to be ourselves. We were needy and wounded, hoping to find in a marriage partner what had been denied us at home. We were sons looking for a mother or artificial and hungry dolls looking for the daddy we never had. We wanted someone to lean on; we were absorbed in an unsatisfying dependency which asked from another what could only come from ourselves. Or we remained aloof and independent in hawkish anger or doveish manipulation — fearing to admit our hurt, our hostility, our inability to relate. The pain of being unloved was transformed into a destructive and elaborate game. Marriage was asked to do what it could never do, to fill up the holes of the past, to provide love for one who had never known it, to build a deep and satisfying relationship from a rigid and frightened role.

Thus we came to marriage with endless, unreal expectations. We projected our own rigidity on our mates in the form of demands and blame and well-defined anticipations. There was a whole set of cultural presuppositions and personal expectations that accompanied our exchange of vows. Marriage was not the creative rhythm of two persons able to be themselves, affirming their own existence by personal honesty and genuine communication. It was not the interdependence of a man and woman who could express their need of one another without demanding compliance, who could move apart from one another without isolating themselves in rigid separation. There was not the permission to be, not the creation of a third substance, as it were, a *tertium quid,* through which a man and woman became together more than they could ever be apart, who, paradoxically, by demanding nothing received everything. It was not discovery but fullness, not freedom, but performance, not the rhythmic release of one's own being but the rigid adherence to a set of cultural and personal rules. It was an elaborate set of expectations which two people poured on one another.

Rick and Ann, married four years, are such a couple. They came to marriage with an entire set of unreal demands. They had not formulated them exactly, they had only implicitly expected that they would be realized. They did not know that their very high expectations would create deep disappointments. Their sexual contact before marriage had been passionate and exciting and uniquely spontaneous. They had admitted to themselves that such intense ardor could hardly last, but since they had not experienced any lack of sexual interest or mutual manipulation, they were only theorizing, paying token homage to the cliché, "The honeymoon won't last." Actually they believed it would last. They had no understanding of what led them to marriage, of why they selected one another. They presumed they were "in love." But marriage brought about at the very start a sudden and precipitous change. Rick experienced a kind of impotence with Ann and a desire for extramarital experience. Ann was tense and bored and found that she was avoiding sexual confrontation whenever possible.

Their marriage had settled into a steady and rigid ritual. Once there had been a great deal to talk about.

They had eagerly awaited each contact during courtship. They laughed easily, shared childhood experiences, recalled amusing and exciting things that had
happened in the past. They learned each other's tastes,
were introduced to different and exotic foods, shared
music and their "special song," did not care where they
were or what they did — as long as they were together.

Not only had they anticipated a continuation of
exciting sex and stimulating conversations, but each
had predicted the behavior of his partner. Rick knew
that Ann would be interested in his work as a stock-
broker — his progress, his challenges, his well-formu-
lated opinions. Ann expected that Rick would continue
to be delighted with her motherly attentions, the little
innuendos that turned their apartment into a home,
her steady effort to please him. They expected hours to
wander, to listen to music, to take vacations, to watch
television, to read quietly in the evening together. There
would be the thrill of saving for a down payment on a
home, the excitement of making new and interesting
friends. There would be birthdays and anniversaries,
holidays and visits to families, quiet and sacred times
alone. And there would, of course, be children and the
delight in offering them love and enjoying their latest
antics. There would, of course, be conflict, but it would
be short-lived and soon resolved.

In reality they had *not* anticipated the conflict. They
had not known the sullenness, the isolation, the mis-
understandings, the loneliness, the selfishness, the

jealousy, the dishonesty, the inability to express one's feelings. They had no knowledge of the dullness and boredom, the sameness and hypersensitivity, the wounded feelings and deep anger. Ann began to feel that she was left out of Rick's life and resented the hours spent at home alone. She had quit her job and found that time wore on her hands, that gossiping women only irritated her. And she had not expected that Rick would demand her attention like a child, that he would be too tired to do anything in the evening, that his sexual overtures would become infrequent. There were quarrels about money, about responsibility, about friends. Many of the very things that were amusing in courtship had become irritating and reprehensible. Rick and Ann are not atypical. Their marriage ended in divorce after five years.

When the expectations of marriage are not met, the couple usually begin to play the "blaming game." After all, the very marriage contract had insisted that a spouse would be responsible for another's personal happiness, for his or her emotional fulfillment. Wives were to "obey" husbands, husbands were to "love" their wives, to protect them, to provide them with their emotional security. The unmet expectations created mutual blame.

A wife could insist that a husband was more interested in his job that he was in her. She would begin to compete for his time, playing whatever game was effective. When he came home in the evening, she was worn out, discouraged, bored. She was lonely when his

job took him out of town, left out when he spent time
with his friends, hurt when he did not praise attentively
the things she did for him, frigid when he took her for
granted sexually, sullen and silent when he complained
about some failure of hers in housekeeping or cooking.

A husband would notice her lack of affection, her
failure to be amused by his anecdotes, her inattention
when he talked about work. He would interpret her
lack of interest in sex as a personal rejection, her careless housekeeping and poorly prepared meals as an
intentional affront.

He would begin to blame her, and she would, in turn,
blame him. The attention of each was focused on the
other. The blaming game began with rigor. She was
disinterested in sex because he was not affectionate
except in bed, because he expected sex without con-
sidering her feelings. He, on the other hand, was not
affectionate because she was always distracted and
chatting about things which bored him. He was turned
off sexually because she merely submitted to his overtures. She went through the motions, she never took
the initiative. She never took the initiative, in her own
mind, because he never gave her a chance, because
there was not enough gentleness and foreplay, because
he rolled over and went to sleep when intercourse was
completed.

The blaming game is vast and endless. It permits a
man or woman to focus all the attention in marriage on
the faults of the other party. It produces martyrs. It

says: "I do the best I can and it is never enough for you. I give and you take, I am unselfish, you are selfish. I think of you, you think only of yourself. You are taking advantage of me."

Our culture makes the blaming game an easy one to play. Marriages are not expected to create conflict. When two people are in love, they think that marriage will last forever and conflict will be easily avoided by unselfishness and love. Indeed, there are genuine difficulties in marriage but there should not be. The successful couple is the one who does not fight, who gets along, who enjoys doing things together. Life should be peaceful, predictable, harmonious. The idealization of human love has become a giant business supported by unsuspecting couples.

In reality, most people marry for the wrong reasons. They marry the individual who seems to make up for what is lacking in themselves. Their marriage represents a kind of dependency, a leaning, what one psychiatrist has called "an A-frame relationship." Thus a daddy finds his doll, a mother her son, a master his servant, a bitch her nice guy. At other times, relationships become competitive as with the hawks or passive, as with the doves. More often than not, they are rigid and unsatisfying. To such couples, marriage is not a rhythmic union, but an unyielding framework in which they play a familiar and ritualistic role. Their marriage may even last for a lifetime. But there is no life, only the sameness of death, only the routine fulfillment of a psychological need. Actually there is no relationship, only an arrangement which sometimes remains comfortable because it is ever the same, or because real contact is never made. Even hurt disappears in the face of depression and quiet despair.

Such dependent relationships or totally independent "unions" are transformed or terminated when one or both of the parties decides to move past the sterile starting point of the marriage. They recognize what has happened to them. They understand the personal need which brought them together and kept them locked in a familiar role. They begin to understand that their very conflict is an indication of their desire to grow.

Marriage has become very much an institution or a *rigid system* of control. When people jokingly say, "But who wants to live in an institution all his life?" they express the idea that marriage has become a rigid system of role-relationships which suppresses conflict and life itself. Our thesis is that when modern marriage becomes an *elastic system*, allowing for open and direct expression of conflict with shifting balances of power, then will it become an expression of pulsating, vibrating life.

Conflict is what exerts pressure for innovation and creativity. A clash of values and interests, between what *is* and what *can be*, produces vitality. In many marriages indifference and apathy result when the two partners, like doves, cease to value conflict and retreat into silent separation. When such conflict can be expressed with anger but without hostility, when the very conflict is anticipated, it is not destructive and defeating but creative and exhilarating.

Conflict in marriage, much like tension in the body, is a signal that change is necessary. But it is not demanded or expected. It is a warning, a plea, an urgent request. If a couple are locked in a tight relationship which forbids conflict, then the marriage usually ends in divorce unless the very conflict, as with hawks and doves, is the fiber of the relationship. A rigid relationship, much like a totalitarian society, does not permit change. There is no ultimate release of tension. There must be a revolution to overthrow the tyrant. In marriage, such a revolution is called divorce.

If a marriage is elastic enough to permit conflict, and there is a shifting balance of power, if a man and woman have the "courage to be" to one another, then a rhythmic relationship results. Daddies and mothers can at times be childlike without rigidly becoming sons and dolls. From time to time they will even be free to appear as bitches and nice guys. At other times a man will enjoy a chance to be a master and a woman to be his faithful servant. Or a man can serve and a woman enjoy the chance to be attended.

Rigidity forbids such changes. Men and women are then denied the chance to be themselves. Weaknesses are forbidden, well-established roles must be maintained, "strength" and "virtues" alone deserve respect. There is no *place for change.*

But if such changes are not allowed within marriage, then there will inevitably be a demand for a change of the system. This is what happens with divorce.

Divorce is, of course, an expression of conflict. It well may be necessary when a couple discover that their marriage is only painful and destructive. Equally as often, however, it may be another rigid solution to a rigid relationship. There is no place for creative conflict so the union must be ended in divorce. The positive power of conflict is not understood. Conflict should be anticipated, not avoided; it should be expected, not decried.

A rhythmic relationship is a marriage which has found its natural rhythm, rather than an institution rigidified in roles. Blaming and expectations are reduced and each person has the courage to be all the parts of himself, rhythmically. Marriage becomes a *relationship* and not an *institution.*

In a rhythmic relationship, which well may have started as one of the dependent and complementary relationships of which we have been speaking, conflict is an opportunity for growth and mutual understanding. It is a new and deeper revelation. The couple, perhaps a daddy and his doll, do not rigidly adhere to the roles which they assumed at their courtship and marriage. The man discovers that he does not want a doll, that she is selfish and dishonest, dull and unimaginative, that she is still living out her relationship with a doting father. She is a manipulator and does not know how to love. The doll, too, may grow weary of her dependency and tired of her protective daddy. She is on display, she is his status symbol, she represents him well. She may want to be a *person*, to have an opinion, to discover herself as a woman. She may begin to resent his manipulating overtures, his need to keep her as a loving pet. Hopefully, there will be conflict, and the rhythm of the relationship will determine if they can grow past the point of the artificial rigidity of a daddy and his doll.

We have concluded from our research that extremely few marriages — not even many second and third marriages — begin as rhythmic relationships. Most of us enter marriage hoping that another will do for us what we have to do ourselves. We have sought out our support. We learned in our courtship, however long or short, to feel safe and comfortable with another person. We need that person, we depend on him, we expect to find in him what is lacking in ourselves. Courtship itself is usually deceptive. It is often a way of "winning" someone we need, rather than relating to someone we love.

Within a few months after marriage, we are given the opportunity to grow. The rigidity of our relationship is threatened. We did not *expect* another person to behave in this or that way. We did not realize that he or she was like this. Usually an effort will be made to beat the offending person back into the routine and familiar role. Often he will fall back into place. Then the conflict occurs again. There is a *crisis.* The superficial view of marriage would say that the relationship is threatened. A realistic view would say that an opportunity for growth is at hand.

Now the couple is asked to communicate, to take the real risk of love, the "leap of faith," namely: "Can I be loved as I really am?" Or, "Must I remain in the accustomed stereotype to receive the approval of my partner?" The *expectancy myth* is challenged, the *blaming game* is opportune, the chance to transmit the guilt is at hand. All the familiar, manipulating lines rise to the lips: "How can you treat me this way?" or, "You weren't like this before marriage!" or, "We might just as well get a divorce." Perhaps there will be a sullen retreat, an accusing and prolonged silence, a permanent pout, a denial of sexual pleasures, a resigned martyrdom, a hawkish explosion or a doveish giving in.

Or perhaps there will be the beginning of a relationship. The rhythmic relationship does not simply happen. It is the result of creative conflicts, or tense encounters which end in deeper, mutual understanding. But only the puritan or his cultural counterpart will call this "hard work." It is exciting, fulfilling, challenging. It is not "worked at"; it takes place when men and women dare to be themselves because all else is role-playing.

The person who has a rhythmic relationship does not play the expectancy or blaming game. He *accepts* his frustrations as personally *his own.* For example, if he finds himself resenting his dependency on the other, he *owns* his dependency as his own need, as his own problem, and tries to become more personally adequate, rather than blaming the other for keeping him dependent.

If he finds himself too independent and cut off from the other, he seeks to re-established genuine contact with the other in certain areas rather than resenting the other for neglecting him. He accepts the fact that what is valued at one stage of growth (dependency) may become a source of frustration at another stage (independence). But most of all, he *takes responsibility for his own frustration* at the moment rather than blaming or expecting.

Sometimes a man will need to be a dependent, frightened, little boy. He does not have to always be strong, self assured and independent. He can be what he is at that moment, and it will be understood or at least accepted by the other. He accepts it in himself as well. Often the woman is ready to be a kind of mother at such moments because she knows that she will not always be cast in this role. It is not a role at all, it is a side of the repertoire of the relationship between a man and a woman. Soon, perhaps, she will be a doll, vain, pretentious, flirtatious, approaching her strong and indulgent daddy. In a rhythmic relationship such a fact is not only endured and tolerated, but actually can be enjoyed. It will not be rigid and manipulative. It will be a woman, being the little girl, revealing another side of herself, being herself.

Most of us come to marriage with abundant dependencies and hangups and childish needs. We have often been denied in our own childhood the love and personal acceptance we needed. We have learned in varying degrees that we are not loveable, that our love is dependent on our acceptable behavior. We are afraid, shy, anxious, angry, arrogant, demanding, jealous, insecure, proud, petty, lonely, ambitious, hungry for love, vain, often in pain. We have learned to manipulate, to seduce, to exploit, to feel immense self-pity. We are complex and often unfathomable. We do not know what we want.

But we come to marriage with beauty and wonder as well. We have known the love of our parents and family, the acceptance of friends, the encouragement of teachers, the joy of living. We are warm, loving, kind, compassionate, confident, generous, concerned, joyful, sensitive, religious, tender, honest, sentimental, romantic, humorous, sometimes exultant. We have learned to forgive, to understand, to reach out our hand, to give of ourselves, to love. We are simple and often naively direct. We know clearly what we want.

We are human beings. We are alive and many-sided like the facets of a diamond. The rhythmic relationship makes possible the revelation of the various sides of our personality. We do not bury our feelings, we reveal them. We do not hide behind our unreal expectations and feel martyred or rejected. We express our hurt, our feelings of aloneness, our needs, our hopes and desires. Perhaps even then the relationship will falter and ultimately fail. But it will not be because we were afraid to try, or because we wanted a spouse to anticipate our requests from weak or non-existent signals. Such anticipation is merely to remain in a rigid role.

There can, of course, be elements of rigidity in the rhythmic relationship. This is to say that the distinction between rigidity and rhythm is not one of simple black and white. We are dealing with people, not machines. People are often weak and frightened, lonely and hurt, insecure and bleeding, struggling and diffident. There are endless degrees along the way. But the amount of rhythm in the relationship determines the reality of the marriage. Where it is largely rigid, it is mere role playing. Where it is primarily elastic and rhythmic it is real.

In the rhythmic relationship there are two interdependent persons who relate to each other with freedom, not two dependents who come together out of neurotic need, nor two independents who avoid each other. A relationship, contrary to much information about love and marriage, depends very much on an individual's capacity to be himself, to be authentic and interdependent. He can both reach out and stand alone. Such an individual *wants* marriage more than he *needs* it. He wants to relate to another person, he does not need to lean on someone to make up for what is wanting in himself. He does not have to hang on to another person, to woo and win the other, to manipulate or seduce. He merely has to be himself, to reveal himself, and in the process to learn to know the other. In marriage he becomes far more himself than he ever could be alone.

Most people enter marriage before they have learned to stand alone. They attempt to learn to live with another before they have learned to live with themselves. They hesitate to reveal themselves as they truly are lest they be unacceptable. To enter a relationship in such guise is dishonest to begin with. And when the conflict occurs, they will either take the risk of personal honesty or they will submerge themselves more deeply into an artificial role. This is the ultimate rejection of self, what one psychologist has called the "psychic loss of self."

Such individuals attend social engagements to please a partner, remain in a job which has lost its meaning, bind themselves to a home or a neighborhood which has only symbolic value, have children that are not wanted, want children they do not have, conform to sexual standards which are artificial, spend a lifetime without doing what they really want. And all of this can be done in the name of love or personal sacrifice or Christian concern. In reality it is a manipulation and a lie. It is a prostitution of love, it is a denial of the ultimate value of life, it is to abuse the very nature of the human animal. And it is to pervert a relationship.

Most of us have been taught that it is selfish to live the way we truly choose. We have been told that it is irresponsible and licentious to indulge our own desires. We must sacrifice, deny ourselves, ignore our personal desires. So we spend a lifetime conforming to someone's expectations of us, or to what we presume a parent or a loyal spouse would want. After a time we do not know what we want ourselves, so terrified have we been to admit it. We have only played a role and built a whole life style and marriage around it. In the process we have lost our very dignity and identity.

In reality, marriage should be a reinforcement of our own identity. In such a close relationship we should be able to be as completely ourselves as is conceivable. We do not have to be everywhere together with our spouse, or we can be. We can eat together or eat alone, we can sleep together or sleep alone, we can enjoy the same friends or different ones. Simply speaking, we can be ourselves. And when we come together in marriage, each individual brings himself to a relationship and not a well rehearsed role.

Rhythmic individuals do not hold a partner responsible for their security or their happiness. If they are sad or depressed, they do not blame a partner, nor does the partner blame himself. He knows that he cannot do everything for the other. He owns his own feelings. He can only offer his love, understanding, acceptance, his own being, his anger, or his weakness when he really feels it. At times there is nothing he can do at all. He does not own the other. He cannot remake a partner or promise the reformation of himself. He cannot be other than he is, nor does he ask it of someone else.

Sometimes the rhythmic relationship moves a couple to spend a great deal of time alone. Theirs is a relationship of rhythmic contact and withdrawal. Stan and Carol are such a pair. They have been married for fourteen years and have two children. Carol teaches retarded children and is creative and excited about her career. Early in the marriage, after the children were born, she stopped working and became a full-time housewife. She began to resent Stan, a senior editor, who spent a great deal of time out of town. For a time their marriage, which had begun as a daddy and his doll, became the bitch and the nice guy. Stan attempted in every way possible to appease Carol. She attempted to control him by turning off sexually, by whining and complaining, by playing super-mother and martyr. More and more Stan withdrew. He developed a couple of unsatisfactory affairs. Finally he asked Carol for a divorce and actually filed. During the waiting period, Carol came to her senses. She saw what she had been doing. She went back to work, stayed apart from Stan and became a person in her own right. She did not look for his approval, did not need the gifts that he offered her as pacifications.

They began dating again and started living together before the divorce was final. Now they do not expect to live through each other. Carol has her own world. Stan has his. When they make contact, they have something to share. When they are together, they choose to be. But they do not have to drain each other, to make demands, to manipulate and connive. They are individuals who enjoy being married, not a married couple who fear to be individuals. They do not owe their lives to each other because they have married and had children. Nor do they owe their lives to the critics who question their marriage. They can rhythmically choose when they want to be together and went they want to be apart. Increasingly, they find that they enjoy their time together. Neither is an anchor around the other's neck. Neither is afraid to reveal weakness or anger, joy or pain. They can be persons to each other, persons and friends primarily, only secondarily married. Their fidelity is not an obligation, it is a privilege and a reality. They share with each other something special and unique. It cannot be easily replaced. But each has a separate identity as well. They can have friends that the other has not met, spheres of interest which the other does not invade. They do not need each other's permission to go here or there. They do not have to plot to spend time alone, to do what they choose to do. They do not have to punch a time clock. They do not fear a change in any routine, they do not live with an endless list of demands. They relate as they really are. Theirs is a rhythmic relationship.

Yet, it is not super-man and super-woman. At times they are petulant and childish, at times helpless and insecure. At times they are unable to share some of the things that they want to share. They recognize, however, that each is an individual and has a personal, human right to live his or her life. They appreciate their differences, they respect each other's style of life and uniqueness. Carol can attend the symphony, which she dearly loves, without demanding that Stan accompany her. She can buy the tickets herself, get a friend to go with if Stan is not interested. He, too, can take the fishing trips and camping expeditions which he loves without expecting Carol to go along. Sometimes she goes, but only when she really wants to.

There was a time when Stan and Carol played rigid roles. He could not be away an extra day without calling her and asking her permission. He was expected to bring her a gift wherever he went, he was expected to phone her at night and to assure her that he was thinking of her. She was also expected to be there when he phoned, to meet him at the plane when he arrived, to accompany him whenever he asked her. Each had defined limits and boundaries for the other's behavior. There were parties which Stan dreaded, to which Carol dragged him. There were business events which included wives, to which Carol was expected to go as well as other events where she was not included and which caused her to pout for days. There was no genuine consideration for each other's feelings, only the whining expectation of manipulation and role playing. Finally, when the marriage was almost sadistically destructive and about to be terminated, they began a rhythmic relationship which has continued ever since.

Stan and Carol required therapeutic help to find themselves. First each had to learn what it is to be an individual, to be responsible for oneself and not for another. Each had to learn to abandon a whole set of presumptions and expectations which he had learned from his own culture. In the process of denying responsibility for one another's security and happiness, each learned "response-ability" for himself. Carol discovered how much of her personality and creative talents had been hidden under her various roles of doll and bitch. Stan learned that he was far more than daddy and nice guy. He could no longer be controlled by the guilt which had bound him as a child and a young man. He refused to be manipulated by fear or guilt or even jealousy and pain. Carol lost her artificial hold on him and gained loyalty and love. He did not ask her permission to be free, he assumed it. Carol, likewise, did not have to obey her husband, but to respond to her own inner self. She could ask for help when she needed it, but not manipulate her husband and grow petulant when the help was denied. Either could ask for a response without demanding it, reach out for support without assuming it. Gradually they became *persons* and not automatons playing the role of husband and wife. The third substance was added to their relationship. Each was *more* himself precisely because of the love of the other who affirmed his or her existence. They did not have to give an accounting to their parents or friends, to their society or its culture. They responded to one another without being responsible for the other's being. There was no reason to be a martyr, a long suffering and self righteously sacrificial lamb. There was no need for self-denial, sacrifice, unselfishness. Such "virtues" were only required in a manipulating relationship. Now they could be concerned, aware, interested, personal.

The Italian couple[1] who runs a grocery store in my neighborhood did not require therapy. Nor do they spend much time apart. They are always together and have a rhythmic relationship. The store is their home, their life, their community. They know almost everyone by name, or at least by face. They smile when I buy a half-pound of hamburger for some homemade chili when my wife is gone. They charge more than a supermarket, but they give more. And when I leave the store, I somehow feel more human, more in touch with the realities of life, more a man. They work every day from nine till nine. They eat lunch and dinner together while they work. And when I say: "You work too hard," they answer, "This is where we are the happiest." And I believe them. They do not work at all. They spend the day serving their friends. Then they go home, have a glass of wine, and watch television. Sometimes they play a game of cards or reminisce. Then they go to bed. There is nothing rigid about their relationship. They quarrel occasionally, often spend time in silence, and

[1]Adapted from *The Birth of God* by James Kavanaugh (New York, Trident Press, 1969).

permit each other to live. Theirs is a rhythmic relationship.

Although some very young couples seem to have a rhythmic relationship, such harmony usually takes time. But Dell and Maria are unusual. Perhaps they are a kind of special pair, but more optimistically they are a reflection of the gentle revolution. Both graduated from college and lived together during their senior year. They are gentle and quiet. Dell is an aspiring architect who works with a small firm. Maria is an artist and has begun to sell some of her paintings. They live in the country on a small farm. They have a variety of animals, a two-year-old boy, and a moderate sized garden. They have a number of friends who seem very much like them. No one has to ask to stay overnight or to remain for dinner. It is understood that they are welcome. When Dell is chattting with friends, Maria is free to join him or to spend her time painting or working in the garden. Maria supported the family for almost a year when Dell decided to do some writing. When the money was short, Dell tended bar for a time. Assuredly they have conflicts, but they are able to communicate and to be themselves. It is a joy to be around them. They represent a kind of counter-culture which is becoming more common throughout the world. They also enjoy a rhythmic relationship. Each is able to be himself. Maria does not feel entirely responsible for the care of the little boy, nor does Dell feel it is his job to support the family. They relate to each other. Either can be strong or weak, afraid or confident. There are no rigid roles, no fixed stereotypes, but instead the elasticity of a rhythmic relationship.

Paul and Sally are in their late twenties and have been married for five years. It is a second marriage for Paul. After a year of marriage, it seemed that their union would end in divorce. Paul had beaten her up several times when he was drinking. Sally was passive and stubborn, hostile and aggressive in a quiet way. She fought back by playing the martyr and increasing Paul's deep guilt. Paul had married Sally, a social worker, because she had none of the abrasive qualities of his first wife, a doll turned bitch. Sally was quiet, humorous and easy going. But she was also extremely jealous of Paul who was very good looking. She felt, but had never revealed, that he had married her on the rebound, that he actually could have found someone much more appealing. On numerous occasions she tried to make Paul jealous, and when he was drinking, he usually resorted to violence. Then for days afterwards he would be apologetic, humble and most attentive to her demands. During this period of time, their sex life was warm and exciting. Then gradually Paul would pay more attention to his business, and Sally would feel left out. The cycle would repeat itself.

After several such conflicts they sought outside help. It became clear that they had not communicated honestly with each other. Sally feared losing him, but Paul also believed that if another marriage ended in failure, it would be a permanent blot on his character. He lived in constant apprehension that Sally would finally leave him. In a way they were continually testing each other. Gradually, each began to assume responsibility for himself. As they began to discover themselves, Paul decided that he wanted to go back to school and prepare to teach in college. In reality he had not liked his work. Sally was more than willing to work as a social worker while he went to classes and got his credentials. Later, after the schooling was completed, Sally got pregnant, quit her job and became a satisfied housewife. They were able to spend time together, understand the games they had been playing, and to enjoy a rhythmic relationship. Paul had dealt with his guilt, his concern over the failure of the first marriage, the disappointment he had been to his parents. All of this he was reliving through Sally. She, in turn, had discovered the roots of her own insecurity, her deeprooted body hangup, her fear of having children, her concern that she was inadequate sexually. All of these fears she was able to accept as her own and not project them onto her husband. She was able to deal with her own hostility, to express her anger, to recognize her continual testing of Paul.

Our research has revealed that in the rhythmic relationship, the couples do not expect "to live happily ever after." They anticipate conflict and see it as an opportunity for growth. They permit changes of power in the relationship and avoid remaining in radical and manipulative patterns of rigidity.

It is essential, however, that they recognize what these manipulative patterns are. A rhythmic relationship is achieved not by striving for it directly, but by learning *what not to do*. Thus we have described in detail the rigid patterns of relating in order that a couple, *made aware of them,* can abandon them in turn to become their rhythmic selves. Our LOVE ATTRACTION INVENTORY offers couples the opportunity to make explicit their awareness of themselves in relationship to another. To Socrates' "Know Thyself," we add, with proper respect, "Know thy relationship!"

But the rhythmic couple are not really rigid even in their rhythm. They know that at times there will be plateaus where a partner may assume a role. They recognize it and are not put off. They deal with it. The rhythmic relationship is *contact and withdrawal* between two people. They can go their separate ways, have different interests, but keep in contact. They are friends. They appreciate their differences, their varied talents, their multiple facets as persons. They can even compete, but not destructively and with hostility. They can enjoy competition because they know they do not have to win. They can rejoice in one another.

Their dependencies (e.g., daddy/doll, mother/son, master/servant, bitch/nice guy) are not rigid but elastic. A wife can be a bitch, a husband a son. But they will not remain such. Nor is their independence isolation and avoidance. It is *for* themselves not *against* one another. Their acting out is an expression of a temporary need which the other party can fulfill, or even ignore without jeopardizing the relationship. Such temporary behavior may well be the need which most of us have from time to time to be sad or petulant, weak or helpless, frightened or in pain. In the rhythmic relationship, such needs can be expressed.

Primarily, the rhythmic relationship permits a man or woman to be himself without dissimulation or role-playing. Each can express seeming negative emotions such as anger and sadness, as well as positive emotions like caring and love. In either event there is contact, there is a relationship, and any relating at all, positive or negative, is healthy.

There are, of course, varying degrees in a rhythmic relationship. When it is fully mature, demands are reduced to zero. There are no demands, rather the freedom to relate. There is not absolute consistency or predictability. It remains an adventure and there are endless new ways to be with each other and to make contact. A rhythmic relationship is often not comfortable. But it is not "hard work." It is a spontaneous "workshop for growth." The creation of roles is often a way of establishing a comfortable relationship. The rhythmic relationship affords the "courage to be," not the production of mere comfort. It can indeed be comfortable when one has the courage to be himself;

but comfort is not the goal. An honest and human relationship is.

In the rhythmic relationship the partners know where they stand with each other. There are conflicts and differences but not prolonged deception. Each can be a variety of things to the other in the course of the relationship. Agreements as well as disagreements can be open and honest, sex is usually free and spontaneous, differences are appreciated.

The rhythmic relationship is that of two individuals who come together out of love rather than dependency or isolation, who remain themselves even as they grow more intimate and involved.

In a sense, it is the very goal of human existence to become fully one's self, to realize one's potential as a person. One must be free enough to be sad or silly, wise or serious, angry, concerned, frightened, aggressive, childish, passive, weak, confident, strong, outrageous — whatever is human. One can be both an adult and a child, one can work and play, laugh and cry. One then has the courage and the freedom to be.

Most of us begin marriage by playing a role. We do not want to, but we are still recovering from the wounds of the past. Gradually, we either settled into our role or, hopefully, began to risk being ourselves. And with this risk, there came conflict. And with the conflict came the opportunity for creative growth, or a chance to settle more passively into a marital role. Perhaps we learned that togetherness is not necessarily contact, and that being apart can actually bring us closer in touch. Togetherness is only contact when we choose it. Otherwise it can be guilt, veiled hostility, resentment, imprisonment, the inability to make a choice. Contact is always good, while togetherness is only sometimes so.

To pass from the rigidity of artificial roles to the reality of a rhythmic relationship is always painful. Change is hard and full of hurt. Rigidity must be unlocked and reduced to elasticity. Often therapeutic help is required. But always there is pain. It is the pain of life being born, the pain of a person emerging from an old and imprisoning womb. It is a man saying "goodbye" to parents and the past; it is a woman asserting that she is worthwhile in herself.

Mother/son, the daddy/doll, the master/servant, bitch/nice guy, hawks and doves — each in a different way has turned a potential relationship into a frozen role. Sometimes they settle into such roles with seeming comfort. But the therapist knows from his experience and sensitivity that most often such roles merely erect a suitable veneer to hide such "unacceptable emotions" as fear and anger, despondency and despair, hate and untold tears. Beyond the roles, there are persons, often longing for freedom and escape, often screaming out for the chance to be themselves.

Frequently, the therapist is told that every couple he sees discover that their relationship is faulty and ineffective. It is even said that therapy itself precipitates divorce. But the therapist knows better. He knows that literally millions of couples who enjoy externally "happy" marriages are miserable and lonely, are depressed and disappointed. Yet, they do not have the "courage to be." Their fear, their guilt, their anxiety and insecurity binds them. They cannot inflict pain on one another and their children, they cannot endure the pain of growth themselves. But they are already in pain. They have merely submerged it by retreating from a relationship into a role. The hawks shout it away, the doves smile it away, but it does not go away at all.

In reality, it is never too late for anyone to begin. Life is our most precious gift. We have it until it is gone. It is not easy to begin again. To start anew is a world of pain and tears, a kind of unique agony which millions of men and women have known. But it is the pain of creation, the pain of childbirth which can rejoice in the creation of new life.

For some, perhaps, it is enough to survive, to endure life, to live it out to the end. Life is only in the future and in fantasy. But for millions of others, life is living here and now. It is worth any pain to find love, to discover oneself, to be free enough to live. Marriage can work, man and woman can relate — beyond the cynics, beyond the disillusioned, beyond the rigidity of roles. There can be — with pain and tension, with courage and love, with creativity and conflict — the rhythmic relationship of man and woman. But it requires a commitment to life, an awareness that life is all there is, a confidence and "courage to be" — to move past the rigidity of safe and comfortable roles to the excitement and joy of the rhythmic union of man and woman.

Replacing the carousel of rigid institutional roles are two alive persons relating in mini and maxi swings of strength and weakness, anger and love. Instead of going nowhere as does the spinning carousel, the rhythmic relationship is a dynamic, ever-changing process of growth.

In the adventure which is life, man and woman can play a rhythmic duet with each alternating as soloist and accompanist, but together creating all the sounds and varieties of feeling which make the living of every day a creative symphony.

Chapter 11

Epilogue:
Man
and Woman

Man's struggle from the depths of the sea to walk upon the land has been a slow and tortuous one. It was not enough for him to share with other forms of life the right to breathe, to see, to move about. It was not enough to ward off enemies, to propagate his kind, to dominate the earth. Man has always wanted more. He tamed the jungles, challenged the oceans, blasted his cities from the rocks and, recently, entered the mystery of space itself. There are no boundaries to his seeming boldness, no terminus to his curiosity, no end to his ambition. Once he made gods of the heavens and earth and paid them homage. He invented patrons to protect him from nature's terror. But gradually he discarded his gods and looked to the strength of his own hands, the power of his wits, the courage of his heart. He knew that the world was his, with its minerals, its fruits, its lonely and unexplored lands.

His life has been a struggle to survive. He sought to prolong his life, to protect his family, to build his kingdom. He pitted himself not only against the power of nature but against other men as well. He threatened and killed his brother, destroyed his home and farm, his city and his children. Tyrants rose and fell — madmen who wanted the whole earth for themselves.

Increasingly it was hard to know what man wanted, difficult to decide who was right and wrong. Each man claimed God on his side. There was no end to his ambition. He talked of peace, and yet there was no peace. The earth was docile, the stars and planets were obedient, the sun and moon predictable. Only man seemed mad. He did not seem mad when he stood alone with his friend. He seemed mad in numbers, in mobs and crowds, in nations and giant armies. Some fierce anger tore at him, some seething ambition, some unhealed pain. Even in his own nation he fought other men for dominance and survival.

Leaders promised an end to war, that the soldiers would return to their country, that the guns would grow silent. But everywhere, at home and abroad, there was fear and terror, plots and protests, grasping and greed, hunger and loneliness. Man did not seem to know what he wanted. The battle seemed more important than its outcome. There was some emptiness in man that could not be filled. No home seemed large enough, no land vast enough, no possessions secure enough. Nothing was ever enough. The fierce appetite that led him from the sea to the land still drove him forward — and in the process seemed to drive him mad. Always some hill remained to be climbed, some mountain to be brought low.

Faster and faster he moved. He flew across the skies, roared across the freeways, explored other lands, vacationed and studied in distant continents. He seemed to be running from his own death.

And periodically in his history, strange and gentle men appeared to chide him for his madness. They spoke of a world where man did not destroy his brother but called him, "Friend." Such men led without armies, ignored title and office, sought no place to rest their heads save where the lions lay down with lambs. They talked of flowers and birds and men who did not store up riches. They talked of forgiveness and compassion, of gentleness and love.

It was a naive doctrine in a world turned in upon itself. It was a childish answer to men who fought each other for dominance and death. They offered no palaces or monuments, no fierce armies or bloody victories. Only a friend, enough clothes to wear, enough food to eat, enough time to live in joy and peace today. Tomorrow would take care of itself.

But few men heard. Or if they heard they transformed their spirit into a cumbersome code which only fed man's pride in its fulfillment. Or they transformed honest words into elaborate doctrines which men could interpret and turn to dogma. The simplicity was lost, the gentleness was gone, the power was dissipated in towering buildings and regal offices.

But some few heard and turned ambition into love. They knew that the only meaning of human life was love. And they sought and found that love uniquely in the honest exchange and embrace of man and woman. It was a love beyond anger and ambition, a love beyond dominance and survival, a love beyond home and fields and endless wars. It was as rare as it was real, but it gave meaning to life that nothing else could give. For those who found it, it was an answer. It was an end to death and destruction; it was the beginning of creation and life.

Man and woman found in each other's arms what man had been looking for since first he stumbled on the land and challenged the other animals that held it captive. Without love there was no life, only fear and appetite and insatiable ambition. Men fought each other because they had never known love in their hearts. They built monuments to take its place. They filled their barns with grain to fill the emptiness in their hearts, but in vain. They raged at each other to resound the loneliness of their lives and the coldness of their quest.

Without the love of man and woman, nothing will ever be enough. In it lies the freedom which man fights for, the peace which he has seldom known upon the earth, the joy which makes him unique. When love sounds his name, he knows that there is no other name on the earth which sounds like his. And without such love, he will spend his life testing and proving, competing and conquering, challenging and struggling to quiet the restlessness which can only rest in his beloved.

For man and woman are more beautiful than all the trees, more beautiful than sky and sun and all the plants that give greenness and freshness to the earth. Their hands extended to one another are stronger than the rocks that bulge from mountains, gentler than the streams that run through forests, more comforting than the shade which shields the sun.

If man and woman find the unique love that can be theirs on earth, then the mystery of life is suddenly mysterious no longer. Without this love, they can only grope and starve, build walls around their bodies and their hearts, tear at the earth in anger and demand that it yield its ultimate secrets. Man, who has wanted everything on earth and in the heavens, who has challenged the skies and even the planets, needs very little if he knows the transforming joy of human love.

Such love does not come easily. Millions of men do not believe it possible, so they consume their thwarted energies in building a pointless monument upon the earth. They beg for the world's attention, they point with pride to the products of their hands. Their energy, fed with the fire of frustration, knows no bounds. They struggle to the end. Or they stop struggling and live their quiet lives of desperation. They cease to ask the earth its rhyme or reason; they cease to ask at all. They amass, they struggle, they yearn, they worry, they challenge, they fight, they build, they die. They have known marriage and children, often enough, but they have not known the rhythmic relationship of love. They have never been able to believe it or they would have stopped in their tracks and turned the world around.

Modern man is living with boundless pain. There is only one thing he really wants from life; to know his beauty and worth as a man, and to hear it from another who knows him as he is. He wants to be special, unique, set apart, singular, the beloved of one as human and beautiful as he. If he knows and accepts such love, then he has known life, and for it he will sacrifice everything else. The gray buildings will not tempt him, the lands and properties of the affluent will not turn his head. Life will be enough, and life is everywhere.

Perhaps man has not really moved far from the ocean which first poured him out onto the dry land. Perhaps the spirit which beats in him, the soul which gives him special life, is only a feeble spark which can easily be dimmed and extinguished. His soul, his spirit, his unique humanness is himself. It is what makes him different from every other man; it is what makes him especially loveable, ultimately irreplaceable.

Such a man longs to give love as well. He longs to take the risk of giving himself to another and knowing the birth pangs from which love is born. Love gives all, risks all, holds nothing back. It does not ask for assur-

ance or guarantees, security or contracts. It does not
protect itself, plan for the future, calculate and tabu-
late. It lets go, it releases, it dissolves. It can live any-
where, survive any threat, endure any pain. It is the
ultimate power and strength of man, so powerful that
even its absence can provide enough energy to build
a world or destroy it.

The world has no meaning except for love. The
world is only a framework in which man can love
woman and woman can love man. It is only a garden
which offers them a million different backgrounds to
experience their love. It gives meaning to pain, to
blood, to work, even to death. Without it there is no
meaning, only the emptiness of symbols and pointless
monuments.

There is no word that a man can utter that has meaning if he has not spoken a word of love. His first effort
to speak, to draw the world from the darkness of life
without a human voice, was only to lead to the expression of love. It was only to learn that he is the first of all
the animals, that he is unlike any other man. It was to
lose his very ego in love, to find his identity only to
share in the gift of human love.

And in the world there is man and woman. Some
fierce polarity beyond sex and blood pulls them together. Some mysterious force seems, as well, to pull
them apart. Some desperate and ancient longing to
survive makes each of them establish contact in rhythmic relating. Man is the sea beating at the earth. Woman

is the land clinging to the silent shore. Man is the night fighting the day for survival; woman is the light pushing her way into the darkness. Man is the sky, woman the land; man is the mountain, woman the fire that dissolves its rock heart and gives it warmth.

And on the planet earth, with its freeways and crowded cities, with its civilizations beaten from the land below, man and woman walk the earth. Some have found love, some have given up and taken security and comfort in its stead, millions still search in loneliness and pain. They keep busy, amuse themselves, serve their time on the earth without knowing what it means. Death frightens them, life escapes them. Beneath their smiles is sadness, beneath their strength and talent is loneliness and longing. They run lest they must walk and listen to the echoes of their own spirit. They sleep lest they know the impermeable blackness of the night. They struggle and conquer, and sometimes win, lest they terminate their days upon the earth.

But every man and woman searches for love till he finds it. He may not even know what pushes and prods him to survive another day. Perhaps love will come to him when he least expects it. Perhaps love will arrive as an unannounced stranger. Perhaps it will never come. But he will look till the end. And even as he takes substitutes, he will still look. Even as he holds out his arms to one who offers comfort and a moment's peace, he will look for the love which might come tomorrow. For that is what man and woman are all about.

Some say that man is all alone, that his aloneness is the price he must pay for his sensitive human mind and spirit, that he only takes a partner to make the journey a little more pleasurable and a little less long. They say that he must stand on his two feet and face the heavens alone, that no one can ever invade the core of his existence and rescue him from ultimate solitude.

Perhaps they are right, but man will never believe them. He will never rest content to be alone. The very power of communication which he has torn from time's mysterious evolving is the special power of life and love. He will share this power with another, he will interpret the earth and give voice to the mute sun and moon, the silent animals and flowers. He will speak for all of life and will tell it to another.

The alternative is the destruction of the earth. The man without love will never have enough, will never quiet the rage at the core of his being, will never satisfy the ambition which robs the earth and leaves it a shambles in his wake. Then there will only be wars and madmen, and empty monuments, rising nations whose energy feeds on those that fall.

Only if man can love woman can there be contentment on the earth. Only if man can study the sky and tell another in a whisper that it is worth a thousand cities and a million nations, can the earth survive. Only if man can look at woman and see in her eyes the reflected love which gives him meaning and beauty can life continue on the earth. Only if woman can look at man and know that she mirrors his own love can the universe continue to have a spokesman for its splendor.

In reality, man and woman is all there is. And that is reason enough for pain and blood and wrinkled hands. Man has paid a price for his ambition to be more than a hungry creature of the sea or a roving animal on the earth. He fought to have a voice and to be called by name. He asks only to love since all of life is love. Now only love will satisfy — the love of man and woman in a rhythmic relationship, which is the secret of life itself and the driving force which brought man from the sea.

Suggested Reading

Albee, Edward. *Who's Afraid of Virginia Woolf?* New York: Atheneum, 1962.

Freud, Sigmund. *New Introductory Lectures on Psychoanalysis.* New York: Norton, 1933.

Gibran, Kahlil. *The Prophet.* New York: Knopf, 1929.

Ibsen, Henrik. *A Doll's House* (included in *Ghosts and Three Other Plays*). New York: Doubleday, 1966.

Leary, Timothy. *Interpersonal Diagnosis of Personality.* New York: Ronald, 1957.

Lederer, William J., and Jackson, Don D. *The Mirages of Marriage.* New York: Norton, 1968.

Lewis, C. S. *The Screwtape Letters.* New York: Macmillan, 1942.

Shaw, George B. *Pygmalion.* Baltimore: Penguin, 1966.

Shostrom, Everett L. *Pair Attraction Inventory.* San Diego: Educational and Industrial Testing Services, 1970.

———— *Man, the Manipulator,* New York: Abingdon, 1967.

Thurber, James, and Nugent, Elliott. *The Male Animal.* New York: Random, 1940.

Watzlawick, P., Beavin, J. and Jackson, D. *Pragmatics of Human Communication.* New York: Norton, 1967.

Winch, Robert. *Mate-Selection.* New York: Harper and Row, 1958.

Index

About the Authors

EVERETT SHOSTROM, Ph.D., is a nationally famous psychologist and author of the best seller, *Man, the Manipulator*. He has co-authored four other books, including *Therapeutic Psychology*, which is used as a text in over 200 universities. At present a resident of Southern California, he is chairman of the Division of Clinical Psychology at the United States International University in San Diego, Director of the Institute of Therapeutic Psychology in Santa Ana, and a member of the Training Staff of the Institute of Industrial Relations at UCLA.

JAMES KAVANAUGH, Ph. D., philosopher and poet, is the author of the bestsellers, *A Modern Priest Looks at His Outdated Church* and *There Are Men Too Gentle To Live Among Wolves*. A member of the American Association of Marriage Counselors and an associate professor of psychology at United States International University, he has a private counseling practice. He has appeared widely on TV and radio and lectured extensively in colleges and universities.

285